Notes on Book Design
by Formal Settings

Onomatopee

Foreword
By Hopscotch Reading Room

We are extremely pleased to be asked to introduce this collection of writings by the Berlin based design studio Formal Settings that offers a fresh perspective on the book as a social construct, with design as its grammar.

Most of our collaborators tend to walk through the doors of Hopscotch Reading Room first and foremost as ardent fans of the printed word. As a bookstore that specializes in printed matter from the non-Western world, this is part of what makes us unique, especially in Germany; a fact not lost on Amanda-Li and Siri, the design principals at Formal Settings. Through our initial conversations about the stock we offer, we gratefully noted their keen appreciation, enthusiasm and curiosity for some of the books we showed them. The first time Formal Settings visited our bookstore, a conversation had begun and we knew very quickly that this design duo were developing a thoughtful and generous approach to books in all of their manifestations.

As booksellers, we've come to view book design as a dance between the words and the reader, with each step and turn crafted to create a fluid experience and a delicate balance between form and function. Through their engaging prose (queens of the subtle pun!), Formal Settings take us through the intricacies of book design and the ways in which the design itself can be a message, a container, and an object of beauty in its own right.

Through their insightful notes, they explore the ways in which book design shapes our interactions with literature and with each other. They demonstrate how the design of a book can create a shared language and culture, a space for ideas to be exchanged and explored, highlighting the social and cultural implications of design. They challenge us to see book design not just as an aesthetic choice, but as a political act with real-world implications; a testament to the power of design to transform our relationship with literature.

— Hopscotch Reading Room,
Berlin, 2023

Introduction

By Amanda-Li Kollberg and Siri Lee Lindskrog

(Formal Settings)

"...the ideal reader, whom books do not tolerate, would know something of what is inside when he felt the cover in his hand and saw the layout of the title page and the overall quality of the pages, and would sense the books' value without needing to read it first." — Theodor W. Adorno, *Notes to Literature,* Vol. 2

People easily get misty-eyed when talking about bookstores—they are highly romanticised spaces. The image of the neighbourhood bookstore that lives in the popular mind locates it in a cobbled street, as a warmly lit space with wet umbrellas by the entrance and the unmistakable bookstore smell. A place where time slows down as you, for a little while, exist in the proximity of the bookstore owner —a being that seems to be at one with the world of books. With their surroundings continuously changing, neighbouring buildings getting torn down and rebuilt, the bookstores of our imaginations are islands, unchanged for generations with the untouched storefront sign announcing its presence.

On our regular visits to Hopscotch Reading Room, we could swear that time distorts slightly, starts bending around us and flowing slower. Its founder Siddhartha Lokanandi has shaped his bookstore into an international gathering space for a diverse community of readers—a portal to the wider world, enterable through the backyard of

Kurfürstenstraße 14, Schöneberg, Berlin. Hopscotch's ever-growing non-Western focused selection of new and used books is complemented by an extensive programme of events (often several per week) related directly or peripherally to books—from readings, discussions and screenings to workshops and reading groups. One such event is what first drew us in: a 2018 Gallery Weekend night featuring a choir singing on the spiral staircase and a drag performer on stilts whose massive ball gown skirt doubled as a tent for guests to walk into for cocktails.

While the evenings at Hopscotch are vastly varied, the days offer time for browsing the collection. No two shelving systems in the store are the same, and it's as though the books refuse to stay bounded by shelves either way—they are spilling out of boxes, piling on chairs, tables and radiators, all in a perpetual process of being (re-)organised, (re-)arranged and (re-)curated.

As the name suggests, Hopscotch Reading Room is a place to read, but it's just as much a place to meet and converse. Neither of us clearly recall getting into a conversation with Siddhartha, it seems to be what just happens at Hopscotch. One moment you are squatting down in a corner to see what's hiding on the bottom shelf, and the next you are in the middle of discussing 70s book design, the merits of a certain typeface or who's in town at the moment, to then realise you have a friend in common in Finland. Through Siddhartha and Erin, who runs the store with him, every book is afforded additional significance in the form of references, opinions, tangents or the story about where that specific copy has been before and how it got to Schöneberg.

Notwithstanding all their literary and cultural importance, as designers, we are often initially captivated by the formal qualities of books. With this as the angle, we've since 2020 been writing the column *Notes on Book Design*, each week choosing a new book from Hopscotch's collection as the subject, drawing parallels between the book as a design object and the cultural movements, political landscapes and economic conditions under which it was created.

The visual and tactile properties of the books—materials, format, typography, binding, etc.—is the entry point of the research. The aim is to understand the role and potential of books as seen through a design lens—to perceive what they communicate through their physical form and map out fragments of the landscape that is design and publishing by looking at many individual examples. In essence: to stare at books until they tell us something. With a limitation of 2200 characters to allow the text to be posted on Hopscotch's Instagram channel, this is also an exercise in brevity. The first drafts, often being 3000, 4000 or 5000 characters long, require a macabre editing process.

As book designers ourselves, we take note of design decisions made by others and try to understand their reasoning as situated in a certain time and place with its own contemporary circumstances, available technologies and cultural currents. The resulting texts are not book reviews, but observations wrapped in subjective and sometimes speculative reflections. In the game that is kicked off as we arrive at Hopscotch to pick out books intuitively and with no set criteria, the reward comes when our initial curiosity is satisfied by the sense-making of the research, and the writing process that follows.

The serial nature of the column has offered a ritual of repeatedly performing the same exercise, which in turn has brought about a development over time. Initially we mainly stuck to observing and describing the formal and material properties of the book, but when reviewing the texts as a collection, we notice a gradual shift to granting context increasing importance. While form fascinates us, it only becomes meaningful when considering the historical, political or social context that has shaped it.

While intending to talk about paper, typefaces, grids and binding, we have found ourselves touching upon conceptual art, the entanglement of language, political woodcut icons, pop-psychology, DIY zine culture, censorship, phenomenology, amateurism as a safeguard for (creative) freedom, notions of original and copy, Soviet alternative building models, copyright protection laws, deconstructivist architecture, and the political importance of independent publishing.

Concluding this weekly ritual of bibliophile sense-making, we now take the project full circle by refocusing on the starting point—the book as object—and collecting 49 of the texts in book form and letting them make new sense with, against and amongst each other. In addition to the selected texts, we have added text no. 50, in which we treat this new book according to the same formula as the previous 49.

Aided by John Seung-Hwan Lee's drawing of the shelves and piles of books in Hopscotch Reading Room, we hope you too sense the value of books as you hold this cover in your hands.

— Amanda-Li Kollberg and
Siri Lee Lindskrog, Berlin, 2023

50 Notes on Book Design

Episode 1

Waterloo—City, City—Waterloo

Written by Leanne Shapton and published by Penguin Books in England in 2013

Typeset in Franklin Gothic and Baskerville, designed by Claire Mason and printed by Clays Ltd on Colorplan bright white carton and 80 gsm Novel paper

This book is a great example of what makes Penguin books, well, Penguin books: functional and well-made without unnecessary bells and whistles, attempting to communicate in the briefest, simplest and clearest way. To us, it seems to effortlessly reflect the search for timelessness that characterises modernity in design. The designer of the book, Claire Mason, told us about the basic principle that guides the creative process in the Penguin publishing house: *"Offering valuable content at an affordable price. A love of the everyday, the industrially made and the accessible."*

The format and the grid of the book are governed by the *Penguin Composition Rules,* the design principles that Jan Tchichold defined when overseeing the redesign of Penguin's paperback books during the late 1940s. At 111 × 181 mm, Tchichold deviates from his otherwise favoured A-format*, opting for taller dimensions which adhere more closely to the golden ratio and fit beautifully in the hand. These specific dimensions are copied from the

German publishing house Albatross Books (see more on page 68), who in turn took inspiration from Tauchnitz Publishers. Under the Penguin umbrella, the format is specific to Penguin Press, the part of Penguin Books that focuses on their non-commercial releases.

Waterloo—City, City—Waterloo is one in a 12-part series about the London Underground lines, each using the colour of their specific line on the cover. The internal design also reflects the story: *"As the book features two journeys, I distinctly remember rhythm and tempo as an important factor, especially when it came to the switch of tones or textual material within the book. It's unusual not to have line spaces when shifting between these things but in order to keep pace rapid and fast, text/voice/typeface rolls on from each other with minimal pause,"* Mason says. All aboard!

16 August 2020

* Formulating his ideas of *New Typography* (in his book by that very title), Tchichold argued that the ordering of elements should be based on paper formats standardised by the "Deutsches Institut für Normung" (the "German Institute for Standardisation" or simply "DIN"). In their "A-format", halving a sheet (for example A1) on the long side creates two new sheets maintaining the same dimensions, in an A-format one number higher (in this case A2).

Episode 2

14 Tage

Written by Markus Miessen and published by Sorry Press in Germany in 2018

Designed by Wiegand von Hartmann and printed by Druckhaus Nomos

From the dawn of the first printing presses, and for about two centuries onwards, typographer, publisher, and bookseller were mostly the same person—or at least, a book was typeset, printed and sold out of the same location. But as the commercial and social landscapes changed, these roles diverged, dispersed, and by now, each of those three job titles has split into a myriad of separate roles (and time zones). There are, however, still many combined titles, and as co-founder of both the design studio Wiegand von Hartmann and the publishing house Sorry Press, Moritz Wiegand is one example of a "Designer-Publisher".

14 Tage is part of Sorry Press' series of visually cocky little books, that testify to the liberation from compromises that being both designer and client enables. The cover composition stays consistent on all the books in the series, with the display typeface and colour combination changing for each one, resulting in a lot of expression, unfettered by a small body. Complementary colours are often paired, vibrating off one another, and everything is oversized and un-apologetic, from the title on the front to the barcode on the back.

Here we spot a bit of a design trend: a utilitarian visual element, forced on the designer, that has been embraced instead of merely accepted. Graphic designers have made barcodes their own by making them oversized, stretched, playful or colourful visual features that integrate into the composition, instead of generic eyesores pushed to a corner in its smallest scannable size. The barcode (like the ISBN number, which has seen a similar promotion from utilitarian data to de-facto design element) also positions the book within a commercial space, as an object intended to be scanned by a machine and sold. The barcode, invented to help bring about the supermarket era of consumerism in the 50s, feels almost kitsch in the waning light of late capitalism.

For *14 Tage* the display typeface on the cover is Friz Quadrata, that Wiegand von Hartmann made a custom, narrow version of.

When you get past the cover, there is only one typographic treatment all the way through: Times, in one weight, one exaggerated size. The images are full spread, full bleed and gathered in one section—a clean and utterly distractionless way of presenting the content which creates an uncompromising and confident whole. Sorry not sorry.

23 August 2020
Images: p. 188

Episode 3
Indien und Ich

Written by Hanns Heinz Ewers and published by Georg Müller Verlag in Germany in 1919

Cover artwork by Ilna Ewers-Wunderwald

Indien und Ich is a 103-year-old window to both a craft and a moment in time. The fact that the spine has fallen off gives us a chance to see the binding, the gauze, and the yellowing glue covering the inner stitching. The book is quarter bound, with cloth on the spine and paper on the front and back covers. It was published by Munich-based Georg Müller Verlag, a publishing house aimed at providing *"High culture to a mass market."* When the book came out in 1919, it was riding a wave of success for the publishing house. In a span of about 15 years they published more than 1900 titles, counting a total of several million copies. This may be the reason the production of this book feels so generous.

Throughout the book, the uncoated pages, now yellowed by years of oxidation, are interspersed with glossy coated pages with photos and illustrations. The cover art is a literal artwork, painted by *Art Nouveau* icon Ilna Ewers-Wunderwald. She was the wife of author, actor, poet and philosopher Hanns Heinz Ewers, several of whose books she illustrated as well. This copy has a classic crest *Ex Libris* on the front end paper, indicating it was once owned by a H. H. Anthony. A whole separate column series could be dedicated to the history and practice of the *Ex Libris* or *bookplates* alone. Diving into that rabbit hole, one also often comes across the phenomenon of book curses. From ancient, through mediaeval and up to Edwardian times, little poetic curses—combined threats and notes of ownership—have appeared in books. Like this one from the 1800s: *"Steal not this book my honest friend, For fear the gallows should be your end, And when you die the Lord will say: And where's the book you stole away?"*

30 August 2020

Episode 4
EROS

Issue 1–4, edited and published by Ralph Ginzburg in the United States in 1962

Art directed by Herb Lubalin. Associate editors: Dick Carl and Susan Ginzburg and contributing editor: Robert Knepper

EROS looks like a book but is in fact a magazine, oh wait, no: *a quarterly hardbound periodical.* A total of four issues were published—spring, summer, autumn and winter 1962—each an ode to the sexual revolution, edited and published by Ralph Ginzburg. At 25,4 × 33 cm, this large, flat publication gives a spacious impression—it's a format for presenting, displaying and sharing. It uses a mix of uncoated, laid-textured and glossy paper and the first issue has a single King of Spades playing card attached to the front cover.

Art directed by the American graphic design icon Herb Lubalin, the layout is simultaneously bold and simple, with every page thoughtfully and carefully typeset. The *EROS* logo was drawn by Lubalin's staff lettering artist, the exceptional craftsman John Pistilli. The letters imitate the classic Imperial Roman inscriptional style —a very intentional way of linking to the classical notion of Eros, the Greek god of love and sex—as well as a way to make the magazine a bit more high-brow. The serif on the title page looks to us like a version of Baskerville with its ballerina leg R, underbite G, slightly laid back Z and wide and open armed T. It's paired with a very neutral sans, that looks in every aspect like Trade Gothic, except the Q and the number 6 (a discrepancy that might just come down to print quality, which tends to challenge typographic detective work).

Just like his almost namesake Allen Ginsberg got in trouble with the law over ideas of modesty and obscenity in 1957 (as described on page 132), Ginzburg also found himself in court in 1963 since *EROS*, among his other publications, had offended Attorney General Robert Kennedy. After four issues exploring the role of desire and sexuality through the lens of history, politics and culture (from a range of perspectives that were more inclusive than those of many other erotic publications), *EROS* couldn't continue publishing due to the federal criminal case against it and Ginzburg (largely spurred on by the interracial photo feature in #4).

A fifth edition was prepared, but never published, and the Ginzburg/Lubalin team instead went on to create two new magazines; *Fact* and *Avant Garde,* each of which have played their own controversial but significant roles in cultural- and publishing history.

Ginzburg ended up spending eight months in prison as a consequence of his conviction in the *EROS* case, but not until 1972—almost 10 years after his initial conviction—as that's how long the appeals process took to work its way through the legal system. The incarceration, in turn, halted the publication of *Avant Garde* which had made it to 14 issues. While the magazine had been impactful, especially in the New York creative scene, it also birthed the widely known Avant Garde typeface, a perfectly geometric sans serif characterised by a huge set of kerned ligatures. It was designed by Lubalin in collaboration with type designer and lettering artist Tom Carnase and after first having existed in a small glyph set which covered the needs of the *Avant Garde* magazine, the set was expanded and a full version of the typeface was released for retail distribution by The International Typeface Corporation (ITC, of which Lubalin was a founder) in 1970.

The cartoonist, philosopher and poet Michael Leunig (himself a controversial figure) has said *"Art, it seems to me, doesn't need freedom so much as it needs courage and love—some would call it soul or Eros."* We would say that pushing boundaries and increasing representation within publishing, needed some *Eros* too.

6 September 2020
Images: p. 192

Episode 5

Metronome no. 3
Tempolabor — A
Libertine Laboratory?

Edited by Clémentine Deliss and co-published by Metronome Press and Kunsthalle Basel in Switzerland in 1998

Typeset with Adobe Garamond. Printed by Schwabe & Co.

The seminar *Metronome no. 3, Tempolabor — A Libertine Laboratory?* was conducted by curator, publisher and cultural historian Clémentine Deliss in collaboration with Kunsthalle Basel. They invited artists, curators, linguists, and mediators into a temporary laboratory for an open exchange of process-based discussions. In that sense, *Metronome* is an organ that is both a collective artwork and a research methodology. *"I call it an 'organ' because it is active, generative, and fragile,"* Deliss explains.

Perhaps this description also gives a clue to understanding her decision to leave the pages uncut. Before the manufacturing of books became fully industrialised, and the printed and bound books had their folded sheets cut open by a machine, it was common that this last step was performed by the consumer. Receiving an uncut book with some of its content still hidden, invites the reader to be an active participant in the production, someone who can decide whether to split open the folded pages, when and how. This confronts the reader, who must also take care not to tear the paper, with the fragility of the material. The manual splitting, usually done with a letter opener or similar, makes the cut much less clean, resulting in fluffy, irregular and more tactile edges on the book block.

The layout of *Metronome No. 3* is an exact copy of a 1968 edition of the book *Justine* by Marquis de Sade. *"This homage to earlier organs is connected to a wish I pursue not to design something new and short-lived, but to capture the energy of earlier movements and recast them within today's context"* Deliss says. Our guess would be that the cover of that 1968 edition would have been quite saucy—in contrast, the elegant sophistication of *Tempolabor* gives nothing away—you even have to cut your way into reading it.

27 September 2020
Images: p. 198

Episode 6

Frozen Tears II

Edited by John Russell and published by ARTicle Press in the United Kingdom in 2004

Cover design by John Russell and content layout by Ruth Blacksell. Printed by Die Keure in Belgium

This note series is about books as design objects, but this week we shift our focus slightly, to talk about the book as an art object and publication as an artistic practice that transcends the walls of the gallery space.

Frozen Tears II is the second in a trilogy of art books, and as such, designer Ruth Blacksell tells us it was important for her and artist John Russell that it worked as an object to be exhibited in a gallery. But *Frozen Tears* is art that is also meant to be read, so it had to work equally well as a book, with dimensions that allowed it to fit into the distribution network, circulate and live on as language. Its 832 pages contain material by about 60 authors, and the dimensions of the book immediately bring to mind a brick, or perhaps a bar of gold. It's fashioned as a pulp fiction bestseller, with metallic gold foil details, and Stephen King-esque horror elements, brought out of the surface of the cover with embossing—all meant to grab your attention from the shelves of a bookshop. 16 years after its publication, it has that precise effect on us.

The content is sandwiched between sections of black pages and there is a ridiculous element to the way large amounts of black surround tiny bits of text on these spreads. The title, then the title again (but now bigger), then an author's index note, then nothing, then just the ISBN and © etc. This effect is very intentional and gives a cinematic feeling—you are hit with one thing at a time, in the dark. It offers a prelude before the book opens up into an uninterrupted reading experience, and closing in a similar manner with "end credits" on black.

We approached *Frozen Tears II* as a book, edited and laid out for a "big read", but its qualities as a sculptural object are equally striking. Around its release in 2014, Russell and Blacksell brought a pile of books to the US for a bookshop and gallery reading tour, but they also took the opportunity to go to the Death Valley desert and build a sculpture with these bricklike books, allowing the sun to catch and bring out their iridescent gleam.

4 October 2020

Episode 7

The Great American Poetry Bake-Off

Written by Robert Peters and published by The Scarecrow Press, inc. in the United States in 1982

Cover drawing by Meredith Peters

Let's talk Bake-Off! No, not The Great British. *The Great American Poetry Bake-Off* is a series of compiled poetry criticism by Robert Peters. Peters was himself a poet who published numerous poetry books, but his criticism and essays on other poets' works are a big part of his legacy. This is the second volume in a trilogy, all with identical design apart from the colour—red has been used for the first one, blue for this one and green for the third. They are designed by Peters himself, and have somewhat of a fanzine vibe to them.

The covers have a playful typographic composition paired with a caricature drawing of Peters, made by his daughter Meredith. The typeface on the cover is a Wild West-style slab serif (quite fittingly named Branding Iron Regular) and no original type designer has been credited for it, but it was digitised and published by Monotype in 1990. It has a funny weight distribution, swelling in the areas going along its baseline and x-height.

It may have been due to technical or economic limitations that the design is repeated on each edition of the series and that the covers are monochrome, but the resulting expression is something it takes designers years to master (and some never do): to keep it simple and hone in on a few, well considered elements that are strong enough to carry the design.

The decision to opt out of the endless possibilities that modern design software offers and embrace the limitations of a single tool can result in bold simplicity. Instead of using professional layout technology, this book is designed using only what the typewriter offers, namely one typeface, in one weight and size, plus underlining and tabulation. This aesthetic probably felt familiar in 1981, but looks refreshing and charming today. Like a typed up family recipe for poetry-cake.

11 October 2020

Episode 8
Suhrkamp Taschenbuch

Published by Suhrkamp Verlag, which was established in Frankfurt am Main, Germany in 1950

The *Suhrkamp Taschenbuch* series was founded in 1971

Following decades of commercialisation of book production, in the middle of the 20th century the format of new publications began to shrink to the point where they could even fit in pockets. Suhrkamp Verlag, like many other publishers, ascribed great importance to giving a distinct look to their paperback books, to stand out in the proliferating pocketbook market. Back then, people who entered a bookshop could immediately recognise pocketbooks from individual publishers, and at Suhrkamp, the designer responsible for creating this uniform appearance was Willy Fleckhaus.

Fleckhaus blessed the books with unexpected and sometimes awkward colour combinations, and a typographic treatment that gives the series an iconic 20th century modernist look. The placement of the solid and tightly spaced title and name of the author always follows a top centred position, with a hierarchy of only two text sizes. The monochrome, full-bleed coloured spines together form a recognisable colour-blocking pattern (or even a rainbow) on the shelf.

The typeface is Times Modern. For anyone who grew up in the era of Times New Roman (which was the default typeface of Microsoft Office 1992-2007), it probably looks fairly mundane, but this one has taller proportions, is elegantly contrastful with intriguing, sharp details. It has some Times New Roman-like features, but is drawn to work as a display typeface.

This systematic approach to designing a series of books perhaps helps counteract the notion that paperbacks are merely throw-away objects that lose their value after the first read. Readers may start collecting the series and consider each volume to have more value when seeing it as part of a whole. Suhrkamp Verlag followed this design system all the way up to 2004. Whether publishers today create design systems that could endure for half a century, we don't know. We suddenly have an urge to start a collection though...

18 October 2020
Images: p. 204

Episode 9

The Lüscher Color Test

Translated and edited by Ian Scott and published by Washington Square Press in the United States in 1971

Based on an original German text by Dr. Max Lüscher

Max Lüscher developed the *Color Test* based on his belief that our *perception* of colour is *objective*, whereas our colour *preferences* are *subjective*—but that these subjective preferences can be objectively measured. His idea was that people's chromatic tastes, stemming from their subconscious, can reveal their true personalities—and that there is a formula with which to make these revelations.

The design of the book is a beautiful example of the Swiss Style movement, which started in the 1950s and likewise sprung out from a search for the universal and objective. Design choices were based on rational argument and mathematically calculated grids rather than feeling or personal expression. Designers swore to Helvetica, which was, and still is, one of the most frequently used typefaces, selected for its functional invisibility.

The Lüscher Color Test has been called many things, from simplistic and complete nonsense, to enlightening and “scary accurate”. Either way, these types of tests speak to so many human tendencies. They appeal to our desire to simplify the complex and find easy answers to complicated questions. Like much of pop-psychology, it can make the audience feel seen and understood, even when one could argue that the statements it gives are rather vague and general. It also allows us to put people into boxes, types and categories, and finally gives us the feeling of belonging to a group by finding ourselves, right there, in a neat grid of numbers.

6 December 2020

Episode 10

Les Nuits de Bombay

Written by Louis Bromfield and published in french by Édition Stock in France in 1949

Paintings by Roger Bezombes. Printed by Petits-Fils de Léonard Danel

Les Nuits de Bombay is the French translation of the American best-seller novel *Nights in Bombay*. This 1949 edition is not just another novel published, but it's a book turned art object. With the textile binding and the uncropped painted illustrations made for the specific format of the book, the cover feels like the canvas itself—as if the illustrations were painted directly onto the book. The effect reappears inside the book, for example on the table of contents spread, where the irregularly shaped illustration bleeds over both pages and almost covers the printed text with its brush strokes. It's also the impressively well printed and vibrant colours that make the paint feel so real.

On the text pages we notice exaggerated top- and bottom margins, marked by a thin line going across the spread, which all together looks quite elegant. However, the justified text (when text aligns in both left and right side) and a preference for few hyphens over good spacing, creates "rivers" on the text pages (when large gaps between words line up across consecutive rows).

So while the reading experience might not be as convincing as the artistic quality of the book, we accept the gaps and rivers as a natural part of the marvellous Bombay night landscape.

13 December 2020

Episode 11

Último Round

Written by Julio Cortázar. First published by Siglo XXI Editores in Spain in 1969, this edition is published in 1978

Illustrated with reproductions of various drawings, paintings, and photographs. Previously owned by the Atlanta Public Library

This book caught our eye from its placement on top of a cupboard behind the counter in the shop, as despite its narrow, pocket sized format, it seemed to have a lot on its mind. The cover reads like a vintage newspaper, a patchwork of type in various sizes, squeezed onto the orange surface and framed in green. The colour combination and narrow margins are, however, a result of this being a library copy.

There is something charming about how most library books are re-bound into coated, textile bound hardcovers. A solid colour fabric with a cropped cutout of the original cover laminated to the front. Uniform, durable, and ready to be wiped down if necessary. With these shared books you can tell, the more worn it is, the more popular it has been. You, and all previous readers turning the pages and adding to the oxidation process slowly yellowing the paper.

Último Round (referring to a final boxing round, in Spanish) is a collection of about a hundred articles, essays, poems, short stories, and sketches by Cortázar, divided into two volumes. The various writing formats also vary in layout, jumping between grotesque and serif typefaces, with some pages turned -90 degrees and some printed in inverted colours.

On the inside of the front cover, it still has the pocket where the library checkout card would sit, reminding you when the book was due. We wonder what made it stray from the Atlanta Public Library. Did it get weeded out and sold due to a lack of checkouts? Did it get checked out by someone who liked it a little too much to return it? Although somebody's library fee might have added up by now, we prefer to believe in the latter scenario.

11 January 2021

Episode 12

Marking The Dispossessed

Written by Danielle Aubert and published by Passenger Books in the United States in 2015

Feeling absorbed by the universe of a book is familiar to most, and finishing a book can feel like being forced to abruptly return home from a rewarding journey. After reading Ursula K. Le Guin's 1974 anarchist science fiction novel *The Dispossessed,* Danielle Aubert wanted to spend more time with it, to recall the lines that had felt profound and contemplate the wisdom she had gained. *"I was so moved by its contents and the possibility of a different social order that I didn't want to leave it."* That drive also led to what she calls *"a search for a collective reading experience."* She started collecting used copies of the book, investigating and comparing underlinings and notes from earlier readers, and stamps from shops and libraries.

Marking The Dispossessed is the result of that process. It's a compilation of about 100 used copies of *The Dispossessed,* including each scribble, stamp and comment that the books have accumulated on their way to her. It's a page by page rendition of Le Guin's original, minus the text, with only the marginalia left. Additionally, all notes have been painstakingly transcribed and indexed, remaining receipts and bookmarks have been catalogued, and each of the covers of the examined books reproduced. It's a book, dealing with another book, on both a minutely scrutinising and a holistically meta level. Things like fake scratches or stamps are usually tacky, but the way this cover replicates the torn stickers, price tags and worn surfaces of various original books feels authentic. It's a materialistic and methodical way to deal with a book on anarchism, an irony not lost on Aubert: "*Many passages in* The Dispossessed *describe possessions as 'excrement'. ... And here I found myself, confusingly, collecting old copies of this book, which I liked so much, and the more copies I had the more it turned into stuff.*"

"Marking The Dispossessed *in a way is made up of marks of possession. ... I thought there was something tautologically satisfying about collecting dispossessed copies of* The Dispossessed." Meta all the way.

24 January 2021

Episode 13

If Walls Had Ears

Edited by Edna van Duyn and published by the De Appel art space in the Netherlands in 2005

Designed by Irma Boom and printed by Drukkerij Rosbeek

If Walls Had Ears is a publication documenting twenty years of activities and exhibitions at the contemporary art space De Appel (1984-2005). When you pick up a book designed by Dutch book design icon Irma Boom, you can expect something unexpected. In this case, the book turned out to be about three times heavier than its size would indicate. It almost feels like you are standing with a piece of brick wall from the gallery space itself in your hands. It seems that the pursuit to embody the gallery wall in the form of the book guides every design decision, from the choice of paper and format to grid, margins, typeface, and even leading.

The typography on the back cover, creating a wall of text with almost no space between the lines as well as the unusually tiny margins inside the book, both seem to us like visual instruments guided by the same principle concept. The idea of walls is also reinforced by the way the title appears in big bold letters around the edges of the book. It's not printed on the outer edges, but instead, every page of the book has a tiny piece of the letters printed to full bleed on the page.

The ability to make books that embody the subject matter and content in uncompromising manners is what has made Irma Boom frequently referred to as the queen of books. Her tactile and material approach to book design often calls attention to the books as objects. Or walls.

31 January 2021
Images: p. 210

Episode 14

The New Radicalism in America 1889–1963 — The Intellectual as a Social Type

Written by Christopher Lasch and published by Chatto & Windus Ltd. in England in 1966

Typeset in Caslon and printed in the United States

The New Radicalism in America 1889–1963 is, as the name suggests, a collection of Lasch's biographies on some of America's new radicals, who reformed American political thinking at the beginning of the 20th century. It was the first book to catch our eye when we walked into Hopscotch for our latest book browsing. The thin and fragile greyish green dust jacket carries a harmonious, centred typographic composition of rust red and black type—an interesting low contrast colour combination that has a striking subtlety to it.

The book is set in Caslon, a typeface that was designed by William Caslon in 1722 and which is part of the reason he is being considered the first great British punchcutter (craftsperson who cut letter punches out of steel as the first stage of making metal type), at a time when England mostly relied on importing Dutch typefaces. He is recognised for the high level of precision in his craftsmanship, and the Caslon design immediately gained great popularity due to its high legibility, organic appearance and classic elegance. Caslon has since been replicated, revived and published many times and is still today a popular choice, especially for book typesetting.

Despite quite a classic and unobtrusive design, we could look at this book for a long time without getting bored. In fact, the title page called for the word "delicious!" to be uttered. The design is an elegant typographical juggle with hierarchies of uppercase, lowercase and small caps, mixed with italics. On the back cover, centre-, left- and right aligned text intermingle in one composition. Even swashes (letters with exaggerated flourishing serifs) are thrown in, and drop caps (single letters that span the height of several lines to mark the start of a text) ornament the beginning of each chapter. The result is a classic layout, rich in finesse. As goes for most typographic rules of thumb, they are usually there for a reason: When in doubt, use Caslon.

14 March 2021

Episode 15

Victoria of England

Written by Edith Sitwell and published by Albatross Verlag in Germany in 1937

Volume 312 of the *Albatross Modern Continental Library*

There is something simultaneously romantic and modernist about this design, with its highly ornamented title page and *Art Nouveau* looking frames, together with the sans-serif typeface and simplistic logo on a hot pink background. It points backwards and forwards at the same time, hinting at some of the significance of the *Albatross Modern Continental Library* series.

Albatross Verlag was founded in Hamburg in 1932 with a mission to publish English language books, untranslated, for the European mass market. They set out to create affordable paperbound books that maintained a high level of craftsmanship, using new sans-serif typefaces such as Futura, and a simple colour coding system: red for mysteries, green for travel, orange for fiction and so on.

The concept was an immediate success, and Albatross published works by Agatha Christie, James Joyce, Aldous Huxley and many others. But only seven years in, the outbreak of World War II brought their activity to a halt, and the founders dispersed. Despite its short run, Albatross is credited for creating the modern mass market paperback, and paving the way for many other publishers.

The unified format (181 × 111 mm, proportional to the golden ratio), the colour coding, geometric sans-serif typography and illustration-less covers are the characteristics of the Albatross books. If all of this looks familiar to you, it did to us too. We felt there was something very Penguin-y about the design; the frame, the solid colour background and, of course, the bird logo. But it turns out that it's the other way around.

Over in England, Penguin's ambitions were similar to those of Albatross in Germany: to provide solid quality at an affordable price (more on that on page 22). When the war halted Albatross' publishing activities, Penguin founder Allen Lane explored the possibility of launching a British Albatross series as a joint venture. When that didn't work, however, Penguin decided to go ahead with their own series, which adopted many of the design principles of Albatross—the proportions, use of colour and typographic style. They also brought in Albatross co-founder Kurt Enoch to manage Penguins' new American branch. The success of Penguin's launch in the UK spurred a trend of paperbacks with bird-logos (the Toucan Novels, Wren Books and Jackdaw Library, to mention a few). So there is in fact something Albatross-y about the Penguin books. Today we learned that the ancestor of that little black and white Penguin on a bright colour background is an Albatross.

21 March 2021
Images: p. 216

Episode 16
Die Spielregel 1–4

Streichungen, *Krempel*, *Fibrillen* and *Wehlaut*, written by Michel Leiris

Published by Matthes & Seitz Verlag in Germany between 1982 and 1999 and printed by Pustet

This is the German translation of the four-volume autobiographical essay by the French author, poet, ethnographer and intellectual Michel Leiris. He started writing the first volume at the age of 40 and spent some 35 years on the remaining three volumes. With his phenomenological and internalised writing style, Leiris invites the readers to come close, as he uncovers memories, delving deep into his own perception.

Phenomenology entails the philosophical study of the structure of consciousness and experience. So how things, people, and occurrences appear to us as we are conscious of them, how we perceive them to look, feel, act and react. As Leiris once wrote in an unsent letter to the French philosopher Georges Bataille about his ethnographic work: *"However intensely we imagined living the experience of the native person ... we cannot enter his skin, and it is always our own experience that we live..."* The path to understanding must go through experience. To us, this approach seems reflected in the books.

The bare-bones design and minimal amount of printing on the covers leave more room for the reader to sense and notice the tactile aspects of the books. One of the titles, *"Fibrils"* (meaning small fibres) seems translated in the various textured cover papers, the four books offering different surfaces to explore, different levels of fragility, different crinkling sounds. The colours of the books create a gradient of earth tones, from the dark brown fabric underneath the dust jackets and through the covers of each volume. Is this tonal gradient a representation of the phases in the 35-year-long process and development for Leiris, uncovering his own memories?

The tactile aspects of a book always act as the sensory entry point to the writing, and this series asks to be touched, read and experienced.

11. April 2021
Images: p. 220

Episode 17

we are opposite like that

Created by Himali Singh Soin and published by Subcontinentment Books in 2020

Printed by Naveen Printers in India

we are opposite like that is a series of interdisciplinary works by artist Himali Singh Soin which includes video, performance, print, sound installation and this *"exquisite pseudo-almanack,"* as Ocula Magazine called it. As a book, it has evolved past documentation, past literature and design, into an experience: an art object. It's printed using lithographic offset, it's hand sewn and canvas bound with a screen printed cover(s, as it opens both ways). It includes a bookmark made from a silver space blanket and the envelope-like dust jacket is sealed with wax.

When we got in touch with Soin, it became even clearer that each material and production method is selected based on what they reference and connote: *"The shape is inspired by an almanack, or instruction manual, the ink by the ballpoint pen, so omnipresent in India ... The cover is canvas, referencing a material that both holds water and resists it, a material that is literally a canvas. For play."*

Environmental aspects were equally important: *"These materials are natural and recyclable, and the entire production is carbon-neutral. It was important to make a sustainable work that did not further the violences it aimed to critique."* Curator and designer Lekha Jandhyala was also involved in the research for this project. Knowing the material intimately, she was able to add to the experience through an expressive layout. *"It was a surprising pleasure, as a poet, to release control of the typography of a text and see what new meanings might emerge with different line breaks,"* Soin says.

As a medium for sharing text and research in an experiential way, the book format naturally complements performance and moving image in Soin's art practice. *"Originally, I moved into performance and multimedia installation as a way to release myself from the page, which I felt was constraining me. Now, the book is a world that can contain many worlds. ... The book is a moving image. I'm working on a second as we speak."*

25 April 2021
Images: p. 224

Episode 18
Giovannis Zimmer

Written by James Baldwin and published by Rowohlt Verlag in Germany in 1963

Cover design by Werner Rebhuhn. Typeset in Baskerville

The design of this book shows a keen awareness of contrast—the contrast between the deep, vibrant blue and the popping orange; between the saturated surfaces of the dust jacket and the almost bare book underneath; between the black casing created by the edges and endpapers, and the white pages inside. This use of contrast is equally interesting where it's lacking: in the way that the title, author, and publisher are set as one collected paragraph on the cover, and in the delicate way that blue initials punctuate each word of the black title printed on the spine, the shades almost indistinguishable at first glance.

In the typesetting, contrast also plays an important role. The book is set in Baskerville, one of the most popular typefaces for book setting throughout the 20th century. It was created in the mid/late 18th century as part of a tendency to push typeface design forward when the traditional oldstyle typefaces were being revived, and sharper, more contrasted letterforms were introduced. Figuratively speaking, but in an all too real way, contrast was ever present in the life and writing of James Baldwin. As a queer black man in the United States during the mid 20th century, writing about race, sexuality, class, and identity was also to write about contrasts. But contrast is what makes us see things more clearly, and for Baldwin, this clarity seems part of the drive: *"Not everything that is faced can be changed. But nothing can be changed until it is faced."*

2 May 2021
Images: p. 226

Episode 19
Reading Scholem in Constellation

Edited and published by Rachel Pafe in Germany in 2021

Designed by Danae Io, riso printed at the Colorama Workshop and bound by Pseudo Press

After *"a year soaked, choked, with sickness, isolation, and racial, climate, and spiritual injustices,"* editor Rachel Pafe hosted a reading group. She paired *On Lament and Lamentation* by the German-Israeli religion historian and philosopher Gershom Scholem, with similarly themed works by other thinkers, to view the topic of lamentation "in constellation". The reading group participants came from a range of different fields and backgrounds, and the content of this book is each participant's personal response, taking the form of poems, essays and more.

The book is printed on a Risograph, or simply "Riso", a contraption roughly the size of a classic copying machine, and the perfect marriage between analogue and digital media. You feed it a rasterised digital file, that gets translated to a physical master stencil, which will let ink through in some areas and not in others. The master is wrapped around a drum containing ink, and by rolling over the paper, one colour gets printed. This lends a half-digital, half-analogue quality to the book, with rasterisation clearly detectable in the type and handmade stitching and binding, making it feel like a zine *dressed* as a book, the DIY-vibe of the layout balanced by the clean hardcover exterior.

The mere existence of any book means that someone found its content important enough to document and share. Books are many things, but maybe most of all entry points to other times, minds, experiences—things meaningful to others. This one is printed at the Colorama Workshop, a community printing studio in Berlin focused on making the production of printed matter as accessible as possible. They believe that publishing is a democratic tool which empowers people to participate in artistic and political discourse, joining a tradition of independent presses in providing non-affluent, non-moderated, non-commercial voices with an outlet. The existence and accessibility of independent presses, no matter how small, are an essential factor if we want true freedom of expression.

10 May 2021

Episode 20

Bécquer: Memoria de un olvido

Written by Julián Márquez Rodríguez. Published and distributed for free through a sponsorship from the Ciudad Real Provincial Council in Spain in 2003

Typeset in Times New Roman, Bernhard Modern, and Brush Script

We'll admit to some snobbery here. When we picked this book up, we gasped, *"Oh dear, this is not ironic."* It had such a New-Ugly-90s-revival aesthetic that at first, we weren't sure. It's so refreshingly devoid of any "rules for good design". On a metallic silver background, a Photoshop-filter embossing of a tree stretches across the cover, and, like the sun among the branches, a feather-vignetted portrait of the spanish poet Gustavo Adolfo Bécquer hangs out around the top left corner, awkwardly close to the edge. On a flap on the front cover, a saturated passport photo of the author greets the reader. Some effects used might feel a tad over the top to some, but following the maximalist postmodern anarchy that was graphic design in the 90s, this early noughties publication is downright restrained.

Since the 80s, desktop publishing has enabled typesetting, image editing and layout, which was previously done by skilled craftspeople with expensive equipment, to be done by just about anyone. The effect that easy-to-use software, alongside templates, automation and on-demand printing has had on the publishing industry is a whole debate in itself, but there is no doubt that it has somewhat democratised publishing. It has removed gatekeepers and significantly lowered the economic threshold. You want something published? Go for it!

It's easy to accuse this book of crimes against design, like the feathered portrait atop the effect-soaked cover image, the Microsoft Word system fonts, the typographic "orphans" (a single word that sits at the bottom of a paragraph of text) on the flaps... But looking at the face of Rodríguez, we ask ourselves: Is this the face of someone who cares about that high-brow nonsense? No. It's the face of a retired civil servant renowned for his knowledge of poetry, who published several popular and award-winning books, founded a literary society in the 70s that is still active and whose local city council sponsored the publication of this book so that it could be distributed for free.

Until just a few decades ago, books were expensive to produce, making the path to publishing a question of either commercial viability or pre-existing wealth, and the access to books a thing for the affluent. That's not the case anymore. This book is a celebration of that.

16 May 2021

Episode 21
Was zu sagen bleibt

Written by Werner Hamacher and published as *roughbook004* by Urs Engeler and Christian Filips in Switzerland in 2009

Typeset in New Baskerville Roman

There is a formula of sorts for what goes where on a book and in roughly what size, but deviations show up—attempts to push the limits of what works, and to challenge expectations. The *roughbooks* series *("Poetry in digital print and for direct sale")* is one example. Number 004 is an extended version of a lecture by Werner Hamacher given in 2003. The layout seems to ask the question: "What is a lecture, published in print?" It answers by deconstructing the book formula and rebuilding it in black and white, one typeface, one weight: New Baskerville Roman with a narrow line spacing, ascenders and descenders clashing.

Visually, you immediately enter a space in which a lecture is held, and at the bottom of the cover the speech is interrupted mid-sentence. It's like the speaker suddenly starts walking away and you have the urge to follow. Each page is set in one point size, starting large on the cover and growing smaller along the way as you move further into the book (like how one's attention level at a lecture might dwindle slightly as time passes) ending with the credits, again in a large size, like a loud ovation from an audience.

The series is published by Urs Engeler and Christian Filips, and the defiance that characterises the layout is present throughout: they refuse any planning, marketing strategies or self-description. When asked in an interview on which criteria they selected what to publish, Filips answers that it has been enough that neither of the two vetoed the idea. Looking back, Filips can detect keywords such as nonconformity and procedural thinking, but says they resist any labelling that could define the series.

However, sometimes they do buckle under existing structures. One example is the International Standard Book Number system (ISBN) which was introduced in 1970 and provides books with a unique identification code. The way the numbers are issued is country-specific; some countries issue the codes for free via publicly funded institutions like libraries or ministries of culture, while others are provided for a fee (for example 125$ per code in the US) via for-profit organisations. Some countries issue them no-questions-asked, while others require the manuscript to pass governmental review or even a censorship board.

Having an ISBN gives access to distribution systems as well as applications for grants and awards and makes the book easily searchable, but *getting* it is where the inequalities in its underlying structure are revealed. Filips wanted to challenge this standard and publish without an ISBN, but since the number opens so many doors, they chose to go ahead with the ISBN. It's as if without it, your book does not exist.

23 May 2021

Episode 22

NATO as the left hand of god

Written by Slavoj Žižek and published by Bastard Books in Croatia in 1999

Designed by Dejan Krišić and Rutta DD (Stereotype)

Aiight (to use a 90s expression): this is a perfect specimen of postmodern grunge graphic design. The book sports a combination of two Emigre type foundry fonts, both created by type designer Zuzana Licko: Filosofia and Base Nine. All the typefaces from Emigre are from, and for, the digital age and created for screens first, meaning pixels dictate every proportion. These considerations then get inherited in the print versions of the fonts, making the fingerprint of the computer visible on the printed page. In 1999, Emigre fonts were everywhere, as intertwined with the 90s graphic design scene as pop pastels and Memphis patterns. The pointing hand icon on the cover, in type terms a "manicule", is historically one of the most common pictographic symbols. Hand drawn versions appear in manuscripts from the 12th century onward, and it became a common icon in print fonts early on, for example appearing in a Garamond typeface from 1530. The symbol is a staple in letterpress print (think Western style "Wanted" posters) and various pointing hands were also included in early computer system fonts like Wingdings, bringing it safely from the dawn of publishing and into the digital era. The pointing hand cursor is a common example of a manicule in use today. Writing the paper type or typeface in the colophon of a book is fairly common, but this one takes things one step further, listing all software and hardware used in the process of creating the book. This further underlines the close relationship between digital and print, screen and page, that informed this design.

The book is bilingual, using all right pages for the Croatian version, and the right pages of the up-side-down book for the English version. Adding title, author, page and chapter number to each text page is already a lot. Then add intro pages of saved-from-the-internet image collage, and you have a book which can best be described as *full on*. But that is the 90s attitude for you. As the cool kids said back then: Talk to the hand. The manicule, that is.

18 July 2021

Episode 23
Koolhaas in Beijing

Written by Edzard Mik and published by the Netherlands Foundation for Visual Arts, Design and Architecture in 2010

Designed by Stout/Kramer, and printed in the Netherlands

This book explores the role of architecture (and architects) in our current time. To us, it seems to simultaneously be exploring the role of the book (and book designer) in the act of discovery and learning. What visual and tactile experiences can the book provide, through the paper visible underneath the text, through the printing conveying the words and through the design, setting the stage for communication?

In this case, every aspect has been considered in order to completely infuse the book with an urbanist atmosphere. The essay *Koolhaas in Beijing* is about the architectural presence of Dutch architect and deconstructivist Rem Koolhaas in the Chinese capital, and uses his CCTV building (or "The Big Pants", as Beijing residents call it) as focal point. The building's characteristic pant-like shape is mimicked in the layout of the type on the cover, in itself a nice deconstructivist touch.

The cover and content are typeset in either Univers or Zurich, both typefaces by Swiss type designer Adrian Frutiger. The font choice lends the book a vibe of Swiss modernism and uniformity that goes well with the urbanism and futurism of Koolhaas.

Grey is otherwise the encompassing word for this design. The book is grey, on grey, in grey. The entirety of the book is made out of dyed grey paper and printed with metallic grey Pantone ink (except for some black in the title that we can call a very dark grey), bringing to mind concrete and steel. The cover is grey, the dust jacket it's wrapped in is grey, even the bookmark ribbon is grey. Despite this, the design doesn't feel heavy or subdued, but instead, rather like the CCTV building, manages to feel dynamic and contrastful somehow. The artist Helen Van Wyk has once said that grey is the queen of colours, as it makes everyone else look good. But this book proves that grey can make grey itself look pretty good too.

9 August 2021

Episode 24
Hobson-Jobson

By H. Yule and A. C. Burnell. New edition edited by William Crooke

Published by Rupa&Co in 1986 (first edition 1886) and printed by Rekha Printers in India

Dust jackets, or dust covers, exist to get crumpled, dirty and faded, so that the hardcover underneath can stay more pristine. *Hobson-Jobson* is clad in a dark blue dust jacket densely sprinkled with example words in yellow, red, blue, green and orange, rotated in various directions in a playful pattern and on the spine the title is repeated, forming a pile on the broad surface.

Stripping the book of this busy and colourful outer layer reveals a beautiful and simple blue textile bind. The confetti is gone, and the remaining pile of words on the spine are now all in gold. Inside, it has all the visual authority of the dictionary: the dense layout and typographic styling that aid clarity and navigation.

Dictionaries are authorities, utilitarian, and give off an air of objectivity. But here, it's all in the styling. *"It's a madly unruly and idiosyncratic work,"* poet Daljit Nagra has said about *Hobson-Jobson. "It's not so much an orderly dictionary as a passionate memoir of colonial India. Rather like an eccentric Englishman in glossary form."* The book is subtitled *"A Glossary of Colloquial Anglo-Indian Words and Phrases, and of Kindred Terms, Etymological, Historical, Geographical and Discursive..."* Or, as the BBC has described it, *"A dictionary of the words that the English owes to India."* It's what happens when you take the language of a colonial power and smash it into a host of other languages with such a force that 1069 pages worth of new words and expressions arise. The target group of *Hobson-Jobson* was Brits living in the colonies, and the book hoped to be somewhat useful but mostly entertaining. On whose behalf is a little unclear.

The title is an example of what the author calls: *"Oriental words highly assimilated, perhaps by vulgar lips, to the English vernacular."* The British heard Muslims in India chant "Yā Hussain! Yā Hassan!" as a part of a mourning ceremony and derived "Hobson-Jobson" from it. The rite of grief seemed to the outsiders a spectacle, and the term came to refer to any entertainment.

These types of "rhyming reduplications" are in English used to signify something juvenile (as in Humpty Dumpty) or pejorative (like mumbo-jumbo), and now the confetti cover is beginning to make sense. Let's keep the dust jacket on this one. It feels like it suits it.

23 August 2021

Episode 25

Grid Bloc

Created by Haegue Yang in collaboration with Jeong Hwa Min and published by Wiens Verlag & Bomdia Books

Cover design by Studio Manuel Raeder. Printed by Benedict Press Münsterschwarzach in Germany in 2013

Sometimes big stories hide between the fine lines of a piece of graph paper. South Korean artist Haegue Yang often uses mundane everyday objects such as Venetian blinds or clothing racks to address ideas of modernisation and industrialisation in connection to topics of migration, displacement and diasporas. While this generally takes the form of installation- and sculpture works, with her *Grid Bloc* series she takes a product approach, inserting her own graph paper books into a market of standardised grids and drawing pads.

Whereas the DIN A3 format with its plain cardboard backing aligns itself neatly to the standards for this type of product, the typography on the front cover rejects conformity altogether. The obstinate letters, with their crooked lines and distorted geometry, look like they were drawn with a handheld computer mouse, far removed from the pencil-and-ruler world of the graph paper. However, in contrast to the front cover, the specs on the back cover are laid out in a tight and systematic grid-based pattern.

With graph papers, we map our data, make prognoses and plot paths in a two-dimensional space, in order to simplify and structure the world, to analyse and understand visions, realities and histories. In *Grid Bloc,* grids are divided into subdivisions upon subdivisions, with new lines introduced to break the 90 degree angles and create dimensionality. With her alternative grids, Yang seems to recreate what we call standard and universal structures. She proposes an alternative tool for the user to map out new pathways and reveal unexplored connections for piecing together reality.

The grid, already predefined on the paper, directs how we draw on it, just like any tool shapes what we create with it. But who draws up our graph papers? Who codes our algorithms? Who shapes the underlying frameworks for our understanding of reality?

5 September 2021

Episode 26

Fanon — the Revolutionary as Prophet

Written by Peter Geismar and published as an Evergreen Black Cat Edition by Grove Press in the United States in 1971

Distributed by Random House, Inc.

The writings of psychiatrist, political philosopher and freedom fighter Frantz Fanon are influential in the fields of post-colonial studies and critical theory. As the back cover of this biography states: *"Nearly all strata of American black society have found their prophet in Fanon."* His book *The Wretched of the Earth* has been called "a revolutionary bible" and many seem to reach for these grand comparisons when describing Fanon.

The aesthetic of this biography is however far removed from the solemnity of most holy books—the design reads more like a record cover. Each letter of the title is made up of a combination of green and blue lines, that are then repeated as dividers on the back. Fanon's portrait has been rasterised and duo-toned, a technique that in no way obscures the done-with-your-bullshit expression on his face.

Evergreen Black Cat, marked with the small cat icon in the top corner, was an imprint of Grove Press, an American publisher founded in 1947 who provided the defining movements of the 1960s and 70s—be it anti-war, civil rights or counter-culture—with much of its reading material. Aside from publishing many political writers, Grove's books challenged prevailing attitudes about sex, and their publications often got them in trouble over matters of censorship and obscenity. At Grove, Fanon was in good company alongside epochal writers such as Henry Miller, William S. Burroughs, Jack Kerouac and Malcolm X.

In 1961, Fanon wrote: *"When we revolt, it's not for a particular culture. We revolt simply because, for many reasons, we can no longer breathe."* The last few words echo eerily the last words of Eric Garner and George Floyd, both murdered by police in 2014 and 2020, their pleas now a chant of the Black Lives Matter movement. Though one could wish it wasn't the case, Fanon is now as relevant as ever.

13 September 2021
Images: p. 230

Episode 27

Copy, right?

Concept and design by Antonia Henschel. Published by Trademark Publishing in Germany in 2016

With text by Markus Frenzl and photocopies based on original photographs by Ingmar Kurth

Antonia Henschel is a German graphic designer who creates conceptual, often award-winning books. For the anniversary of the BACKENZAHN™ (German for molar tooth) stool by the furniture company e15, she created this homage to the stout little object. Henschel frames the premise of her book as a question: a two-word sentence (and wordplay) that calls attention to notions of original and copy, rendition and authenticity. The BACKENZAHN™ is one of e15's most iconic designs. Each leg is carved from the centre of a tree, which gives a lot of variation in patterns, making every stool unique. In the book, no images of the actual stools are shown, per se—only photocopies (reproductions) of photographs (reproductions) of the individual (unique) specimen.

The screen print on the cover is rough, like it was also produced on a copying machine. The book is set with a textbook version of Helvetica, functional and neutral, but with a one-story a, straight t and stemless u, providing an added naiveté. By justifying the paragraphs throughout (even when that creates gaps between the words) Henschel makes the text blocks relate to the shape of the stool: straight edges on the outside, with space instead distributed within. The placement and composition of the images are repetitive, but in this repetition we are made to notice the more subtle variations of texture and light as rendered via the grainy photocopies. Through this rough presentation, the iconic design is somehow made abstract—made into platonic copies of copies of the pure BACKENZAHN™ ideal.

Something more traditional or polished would probably not have befitted this stool. *"The BACKENZAHN™ is not a light, graceful piece of furniture,"* Frenzl writes, *"... it asserts itself with its materiality, the cracks in the wood, defiantly, next to more elegant furniture, polished surfaces, fine fabrics or materials that are free from defects. ... It's a piece of naturalness and authenticity that exposes all chichi to ridicule."*

20 September 2021
Images: p. 234

Episode 28

National Letters: Languages and Scripts as Nation-building Tools

Edited and designed by Marek Nedelka and published by Letter Books in the Czech Republic in 2021

Typeset with Stempel Garamond and Neue Haas. Printed by Quatro Print

In *National Letters*, Czech designer and editor Marek Nedelka invites international contributors to give their input on the topic of script and language and how these influence our lives. Their entry points are varied: linguistics, anthropology, history, political science, sociology, and philosophy. Through four case studies, the book investigates the so-called "national scripts" of Israel, Georgia, Turkey, and Ethiopia. The harmonic layout and well-crafted typesetting make the expression both contemporary and timeless, effortlessly balancing function and beauty.

On the cover, the title is set in five different scripts. The focused and clear composition is blind embossed (raised, with no print) and on the dust jacket, the English title has black print added. The embossing adds a tactile dimension to the book, and is also, according to Nedelka, a nod to the Rosetta Stone and the concept of translation/transliteration. The design becomes an experience of light and angles, of feeling with your fingers as much as seeing with your eyes. The uncoated 80 gsm content pages are interspersed with small sections of thin (60 gsm), coated stock, where full bleed photographic material act as dividers between each section that become visible as thin lines along the edges of the book block. The light paper is a deliberate choice: by keeping the format lightweight and small, both production and shipping become more affordable and the book therefore more accessible.

Nedelka is also the founder of Letter Books, *"a small publishing imprint focusing on language, writing systems and typography to get deeper into reading letters from unexpected directions." National Letters* is its first title, but more are in progress—their next title *Mysterious Letters* is set to come out in the summer of 2023. With its strikingly understated design, *National Letters* seems to say: Language is both visible and tactile, and needs to be both seen and felt.

28 September 2021
Images: p. 240

Episode 29

Locus Solus I–IV

Edited by H. Mathews, J. Ashbery, K. Koch and J. Schuyler and published by Locus Solus Press in France in 1961–62

Printed as a limited edition of 50 copies by Atar S. A. in Switzerland

Locus Solus was a short-lived journal of experimental poetry and prose. Each issue was between 150 and 300 pages, ca. 13 × 18 cm in format and stitched—a magazine shaped like a book. The cover papers have mild colours (softened even further with time), each issue with a different texture—one is coated, another is like craft paper, and the third is a thin "laid paper" (with stripes resulting from the manufacturing process showing in the fibrous surface). A total of five issues of *Locus Solus* were published before the project was shelved.

Behind the publication were members of the so-called New York School, an informal group of American poets, painters, and other creatives active in the 1950s and 60s. Aside from the editors, contributors included André Breton, William S. Burroughs, Gregory Corso and many others. The group was inspired by surrealism, abstract expressionist art and experimental music among other boundary-pushing movements, yet the layout of *Locus Solus* shows both restraint and clarity. The aim of the journal was to share high-quality literature and poetry in a simple and elegant way, produced and distributed with care and respect. It's harmoniously typeset and has a lot of detail and variation without losing clarity.

The name "Locus Solus" was borrowed from a novel by Raymond Roussel from 1914 and has the double meaning of a solitary and a unique place. The rhyming, poetic words seem to appeal to many and are also the title of a sound performance by a Slovenian artist, an annual music festival in France and a spaceship in a sci-fi video game. To describe the *Locus Solus* at hand, however, we'll give the last word to writer Jed Birmingham: *"(these publications) are yet another example of the magazine as alternative space. ... I see* Locus Solus *as a form of* Kunstkammer *(a Cabinet of Wonder), a closed hermetic space akin to Cornell's and Duchamp's boxes. A closed space, yet one that opens into an endless labyrinth of choices, options, and possibilities."*

18 October 2021

Episode 30

From the Ashes — Voices of Watts

Edited by Budd Schulberg and published by The New American Library in the United States in 1967

Dust jacket design by Alex Tsao

After devastating riots and confrontations between police and residents of the Watts neighbourhood in Los Angeles in 1965, screenwriter Budd Schulberg founded the "Watts Writers Workshop" as a way to help give voice to the residents. This first anthology of the participants' essays, alongside a documentary and two subsequent books, ensured continuous attention from the press as well as support from many prominent literary and political figures.

On the opening spread, Ohm's law has been printed as a witty but pointed preface to the texts—it's made clear that the conductive potential of words and the importance of resistance are the purpose of this publication. This is underlined with colour on the cover: bold red and black typography is set on a warm yellow background. The title is set with Pistilli Roman, a display typeface drawn in French Didot style, with a sharpness and high contrast of the letterforms that almost lead the thoughts to flames. Underneath the dust jacket, the half bind is made up of vibrant red fabric and black paper, dividing the surface down the middle. Text is kept on the spine, letting the politically charged colour combination speak for itself. The visual voice is amplifying the content, calling to action whilst telling stories of people whose emotions range from anger and grief to affirmation and courage.

From the Ashes imagines the writers' voices as single candles that could potentially light thousands more. *"And the light and warmth of these candles may help redeem and regenerate the core of the ghetto ... waiting either for a phoenix to rise from the ashes, or for bigger and more terrible fires."* Hopeful words—but also eerily prophetic. After eight years of activity, the workshop lost its federal funding and its building was burned to the ground by a hostile FBI informant that wanted to make sure its endeavours would end. He might have burned the building, but the power of the voices that the project had enabled was a phoenix which had already taken flight.

1 November 2021

Episode 31

Fin-De-Siècle Vienna — Politics and culture

Written by Carl E. Schorske and published by Vintage Books in the United States in 1981

First published by Alfred A. Knopf, Inc. in 1981. Cover artwork by Gustav Klimt

Though from the 1980s, the book borrows its aesthetic from the years around the "Fin-De-Siècle", the end of the 19th century. This period, also described as the *Wiener Moderne* era, was one of fast socio-political development and weakening authority of history in favour of a growing interest in the future. The political climate in Europe (a failure of liberalism paired with growing nationalism and anti-semitism) as well as the emergence of psychoanalysis, the Marxist movement and industrialisation, were all at play in this turbulent time. Through seven chapters, cultural historian C. E. Schorske investigates the interrelationships between these developments and key artists of the time. The cover features a lithographic print by Gustav Klimt, framed on a golden background together with the title, which is typeset in sweeping, playfully ligatured *Jugendstil* lettering. Klimt initially designed the print as a cover for the magazine *Ver Sacrum* which was influential in advancing graphic design, typography, illustration, and book culture in general. It was published by the Vienna Secession, a group of artists with a modern and experimental view on both fine and applied arts. In the first issue it reads: *"Our aim is to awaken, encourage and propagate the artistic perception of our time. ... We have dedicated ourselves with our whole power and future hopes, with everything that we are to the Sacred Springtime."*

This atmosphere of springlike rebirth and youthful rebellion was the prerequisite of the *Jugendstil* (the Austrian *Art Nouveau*), with its motto: *"To each era its art. To art its freedom."* Each creative field, be it architecture, art or design, turned its back on the historical and academic and went on a search for new self-definitions. The style is exuberant and full of organic shapes, gold leaf, ornamentation, decorative borders and swirly typography. Today, 120 years removed, it's easy for us to view this era as just another chapter in history. But to the people active at the time, the radical shift from ancient to modern marked not only the end of the century, but the end of history.

15 November 2021

Episode 32
Münchhausen Erzählt

Written by Gottfried August Bürger and published as a part of the *Universal Bibliothek* series by Verlag Philipp Reclam jun. in the German Democratic Republic (DDR) in 1983

Designed by Irmgard Horlbeck-Kappler. Typeset in Garamond Antiqua

The Reclam publishing house was established in Leipzig in 1828 by Philipp Reclam, with an aim to offer literary classics at an affordable price. This concept was much aided by a new law passed in 1867, which limited the copyright protection period of German authors to 30 years after their death, thereby putting a wealth of German classics into the public domain overnight. With all this available material, plus an in-house print production, Reclam was able to start the *Universal Bibliothek* series: quality literature in cheap paperbacks with a uniform design. A newspaper wrote at the time that these editions *"with their nice print quality and handsome design, combined with their inexpensive price, surpass anything a country has brought out on the book market until now."*

In the early 1900s, Reclam started using vending machines to distribute books in busy public spaces and the books were often used in schools, all of which contributed to the spread of the series among generations of people. In 1943, the publishing house was badly bombed and the political climate made it increasingly difficult to continue independent publishing work in Leipzig. Part of the company was expropriated by the East German government and the owner, Phillip Reclam's grandson, moved to the West to set up a new branch. This led to a long period of division during the DDR years.

The design of the series has been updated several times throughout the years, though always remaining mainly typographic. This book has the "Type 4" design, hailing from the DDR branch of the publishing house. "Universal Bibliothek" is set with Super Grotesk, a typeface designed by German type designer Arno Drescher and one of the most frequently used in the DDR. The bold sans serif is framing and contrasting the loosely spaced italic Garamond in a list-like composition, its airiness juxtaposed by the unpretentious wall of blurb on the back cover.

After the reunification, the Leipzig branch was reprivatised by Reclam and the DDR era design was replaced by the more restrained yellow and black layout developed at the Western branch. Today, Reclam is still an active, family-owned business, 194 years, a few wars and some 600 million copies later, and mainly famous for the “little yellow books” of the *Universal Bibliothek*. To us, however, the design coming out of Leipzig in the 70s is the true visual high-water mark for this series.

23 November 2021
Images: p. 244

Episode 33

Some Writers Can Give You Two Heartbeats

Edited by Tinashe Mushakavanhu and Nontsikelelo Mutiti and published by Black Chalk & Co. in the United States in 2019

Designed by Preston Thompson with art direction by Nontsikelelo Mutiti. Printed in Belgium

Writer and scholar Tinashe Mushakavanhu and visual artist and educator Nontsikelelo Mutiti are the two brains behind the creative agency Black Chalk & Co. Their earlier project, *Reading Zimbabwe,* is a digital platform for archiving Zimbabwean literature while also interrogating the power dynamics of the publishing world and understanding Zimbabwe through its stories. *Some Writers Can Give You Two Heartbeats* looks at the voices behind these stories, bringing together some 150 Zimbabwean writers, editors, academics, and publishers into a conversation about writing itself.

The title is borrowed from writer Yvonne Vera: *"Some writers can give you two heartbeats—one for the beauty of the words, another for the event. I want to be a writer who can give you the illusion that you have two hearts."* And the idea of duality is very present in this design. The duotone print (a reddish brown representing the clay of Zimbabwe's terrain, paired with a vibrant yellow referencing the national flag) aids the sense of a common history and vocation among the writers, by visually tying the varied sources together in a cohesive whole. The design becomes a narrating voice, guiding us through the material. *"The large page numbers added dynamism to the book, which allowed the reader to navigate the book more easily,"* designer Preston Thompson says. *"The book can be considered a meta–narrative, and the table of contents on the cover allows readers to enter the book at different parts. It doesn't have to be read in order, and I wanted the large page numbers to reinforce that idea, while adding tension and excitement."*

In an interview, Mutiti reflects on the role of books within education and reproduction of culture in colonised Zimbabwe: *"Engagement with the book, with reading, and with study was tied to unlearning—you were learning one culture to unlearn another."* This book is fully switching the perspective back, letting Zimbabwe speak for itself, with all the duality that may entail.

30 November 2021
Images: p. 248

Episode 34

Howl and Other Poems

Written by Allen Ginsberg and published as a part of *The Pocket Poet Series* by City Lights Books in the United States in 1956

Edited by Lawrence Ferlinghetti and Nancy J. Peters

The City Lights publishing house and bookshop was established in 1953 as America's first all-paperback bookshop, and their affordable editions of world literature and progressive political writings quickly made the store a hit among the broke and woke Beat crowd. In 2001, the store was made an official historic landmark for *"playing a seminal role in the literary and cultural development of San Francisco and the nation."*

The Pocket Poets Series was started in 1955 by City Lights co-founder Lawrence Ferlinghetti, borrowing the design concept from Kenneth Patchen's book *An Astonished Eye Looks Out of the Air.* Visually, however, the *Pocket Poet* books are more elaborate and refined with their combination of symmetry and asymmetry and a stunning typesetting that pairs the 1930s typeface Albertus Nova with a roman Baskerville.

After hearing Allen Ginsberg read his poem *Howl* at a gallery, Ferlinghetti immediately offered to publish it. It was provocative and raw, depicting drug use and homosexuality, and Ferlinghetti suspected it might get them in trouble. And soon, an obscenity prosecution came. Police raided the store and Ferlinghetti was arrested, but when the verdict came down, it declared that the poem's redeeming social value merited it First Amendment protection. This verdict established a precedent that lifted the ban on many important literary works. The media attention from the legal case stimulated national interest in both Ginsberg and the City Lights store, and today over a million copies of *Howl* have been sold.

Attempting to hide, remove or censor information can have the unintended effect of increasing awareness of, interest in and demand for that information. We can thank this mechanism for some of the impact that *Howl* had on what could be said, who could be represented and what norms could be challenged in print. It was one battle won in a war that is very much still raging.

11 December 2021
Images: p. 252

Episode 35

Kollektiv für socialistische Bauen: Proletarische Bauausstellung 1931

Edited by Jesko Fezer, Martin Hager, Christian Hiller, Alexandra Nehmer and Philipp Oswalt and co-published by Haus der Kulturen der Welt and Spector Books in Germany in 2015

Designed by Matthias Görlich

Through a mix of original documents and contemporary statements, this publication looks back at the *Proletarian Building Exhibition*, which was put together by the revolutionary Collective for Socialist Architecture in Berlin in 1931. The exhibition was conceived as a riposte to the larger, bourgeois *Deutsche Bauausstellung*. While the latter displayed a flattering image of the modernist building ideals, the proletarian counterpart shone a light on the catastrophic reality of the housing situation in larger cities and questioned whether solutions could be found within a capitalist system.

The group looked to the Soviet Union for alternative building models, and the architectural landscape they would have seen there might have a thing or two in common with this design: functional, structured, modest and unembellished, full of straight lines.

The title wrapping around to the flap seems to underline the book's architectural properties: with its cover folded out, the publication becomes a high-rise, the muted purple reminiscent of concrete. A strictly facilitated grid divides the pages into neat, unwavering columns, varied in width but with the same underlying structure.

Both of the typefaces that are used are from the foundry Grilli Type. GT Eesti (used on the cover) is a contemporary interpretation of a Soviet geometric sans serif, using books from Soviet-occupied Estonia as a starting point. Inside, the serif GT Sectra has been used for both headlines and reading text. Sectra is also a modernly constructed typeface, combining the disciplined craftsmanship of broad nib pen calligraphy with the sharpness of a scalpel knife. Each, in their own way, adds to the strict tonality that makes this layout frame its content so well. Quadratisch (or at least Kantig). Praktisch. Gut.

19 December 2021

Episode 36
Amateur

Edited by Emily Pethick and Wendelien van Oldenborgh with David Morris and co-published by Sternberg Press, The Showroom and If I Can't Dance, I Don't Want To Be Part Of Your Revolution in 2014

Designed by Julia Born assisted by Malin Gewinner and printed by DZA Druckerei zu Altenburg in Germany

Amateurism (as opposed to professionalism) as a safeguard for (creative) freedom is at the core of the practice of video and installation artist Wendelien van Oldenborgh. Her art is often happening with, and in relation to others, the collaboration allowing vulnerability and experimentation to take the place of routines and efficiency. *"For me, this is also an attitude of resistance towards the demand for entrepreneurial smartness, which is inherent to the current neo-liberal condition, the art world being no exception."*

The content is curated in the same collaborative way, featuring commissioned essays inspired by van Oldenborgh's major works. The design captures this meeting between artist and contributors, text and film, rough and polished, digital and analogue. On the cover, the crop of the text box makes it look like a manuscript clipping, pasted in from somewhere else. Below, illustrated strips of tape hold up a photograph, hinting at physicality, while the generated .tif file name speaks to the presence of the digital, even in analogue techniques.

Inside, a skilful utilisation of the grid lets text columns stretch and shift, mixing different paragraph widths and drop-shadowed quotes with vertical chapter titles and footnotes into a varied and ambitious text layout. The black and white essay pages are interspersed with brightly saturated colour sections, cut through the middle horizontally to create half pages that can be combined and recombined, allowing the curation to be interactive and never fully set.

This playfulness and interactivity is characteristic for van Oldenborgh's work: the construction of situations that invite the subjectivity and participation of others. In an art world that has to reckon with commodification and sellability, an amateur mindset is liberating. As an amateur, you don't owe anyone anything—and the key to becoming a deliberate amateur might, as van Oldenborgh suggests, be the vulnerability of co-creation.

16 January 2022
Images: p. 256

Episode 37
Die Haut

Written by Curzio Malaparte and published by Stahlberg Verlag in Germany in 1950

Cover design by Roland P. Litzenburger

When books are published in new editions or in new countries, they also usually get a new cover design befitting current visual trends, local preference and individual style of the publisher. Books that are in essence the same on the inside can look very different on the outside from edition to edition. The novel *La Pelle* (in German *"Die Haut")* is no exception. Its themes of morality post World War II have been interpreted typographically and through illustration; as a soldier intrigued by a lady on a mid-century American pulp copy and as metaphorical birds and prison bars on a recent Serbian edition. Its title has been set in ultra-condensed sans serifs, in Didones, in Wild West-style slab serifs and in horror film brush script. The atmosphere of the story is framed differently in 1952, in 1986 and in 2017.

This German version from 1950 is striking in its darkness. A slight embossing is used to increase the contrast between black ink and naked paper, with the woven tape on the spine adding another texture into the tactile mix. It has the atmosphere of a Rorschach test where an eerie motif has emerged. On the back, it becomes clear that this is as much an artwork as a cover design: the publisher's monogram has become a pendant on a string that twists into a signature: *Roland.* The German artist, sculptor and occasional graphic designer Roland P. Litzenburger was exhibited nationally and internationally for over 30 years. He mostly painted Christian themes, full of tiny lines and detail, which makes this more abstract, inkblot artwork even more noteworthy.

When this book first came out, it was deemed heretical and contrary to morality, and placed on the Catholic's *Index Librorum Prohibitorum* ("List of Prohibited Books"). But societal values are culturally varied and fluid over time, which is beautifully reflected in the way book design changes when stories age, travel and are seen through new eyes. One reader sees a soldier, another a ghost. It's all interpretation.

23 January 2022

Episode 38

Future Palestine

Edited by Amira Asad and Rashed Al Deiri and published by LIFTA Volumes in Mexico in 2020

Designed by Leila Peinado with cover title design by Ahmad Aiyad

"How much of history, reality, and experience can we shed in the realm of the imaginary?" Writers, poets, architects, researchers, and artists from Palestine and its diaspora respond to this question, posed by the multidisciplinary platform LIFTA, in their publication *Future Palestine.* The contributors touch upon an array of themes, from archaeology and sci-fi to mental health and gender issues. "Future Palestine *is a step away from the past and present, from the limitations of current affairs, memory, and rhetoric—a step towards intangible possibilities and impossibilities,"* the publishers write.

The cover of this perfect bound paperback has a trippy, distorted wood-like texture with gold foil embossing on the front cover. On the spine, the English title has been turned into a pattern, like a chant, and the content layout has a kind of 90s, early internet vibe with lots of drop shadow effects. A combination of black and red is used throughout the design, feeling sometimes harsh, sometimes softer, tying different visual expressions together and bringing to mind other movements that deal with similar anti-capitalist and anti-imperialist topics. Repetition, slicing, collaging and distorting are used in various ways, presenting no clear image of the Palestine future.

"Palestine is not just a geographical location anymore," LIFTA co-founders Asad and Peinado said in an interview with Printed Matter. With its internationalist scope, this publication is giving voice to Palestinians spread across the globe, who are living vastly different lives but are joined by a common descent and by a sense of having been radicalised by the same stories. *Future Palestine* aims to connect as well as disrupt, to foster discussions around emancipation and liberation that the readers can mirror themselves in and rally around, the book becoming a vessel for shared experiences and patchworked visions.

6 February 2022

Episode 39

Neues Lotes Folum — Zeitschrift für die Poésie und die Revolution

Written and published pseudonymously or under various fictitious group names by Helmut Höge in Germany in 1975

First issue, edited and published by the "Necrophiliacs Liberation Front Editors Collective"

You have read three paragraphs and already encountered the words "revolution", "liberation" and "collective". Yep, we are in the 70s. *Neues Lotes Folum* was an early publication experiment put out pseudonymously by the German journalist and writer Helmut Höge, during his years as a bored and disgruntled student. *"From time to time I took LSD and at some point I started to take notes. Then I thought to myself, you could make a magazine,"* he says in an interview. The result is a patchwork of heavily footnoted and digressive texts, comics, and illustrations by Höge and other left wing writers, influenced by the likes of Deleuze, Foucault and the French Situationists.

Typographically, the outside and the inside of this magazine have very different tonalities. On the cover, several weights of the geometric sans serif Kabel are used, whose constructed design is inspired by modernist ideals proliferated by the Bauhaus school in the 1920s. The subtitle *"Zeitschrift für die Poésie und die Revolution"* is set in Grotesque no. 9, a narrow sans serif that was first released in 1906, and which has subsequently been digitised by contemporary foundries. While the cover is professionally typeset on a tasteful metallic copper background, the content is straight out of DIY zine culture. The content page layout was done by Höge himself, giving it a spontaneous, unmoderated quality. No need for a designer to interpret, structure or polish anything, or for any professional tools—a typewriter, scissors, and glue will do just fine.

After three editions, the project was discontinued and Höge moved on to other literary endeavours. Today he is primarily known as a writer and editor of the progressive German newspaper *Die Tageszeitung,* to which he has been contributing for over 40 years. The writer grew older, but the core ideals remained constant. *Neues Lotes Folum* is a historical snapshot, an image of an unruly student in the family album of German leftist publishing.

20 February 2022
Images: p. 262

Episode 40

Mulberry Tree Press — Partial Fictions

Edited by Nicolas de Oliveira and Ben Cain and published by Mulberry Tree Press in England in 2011

Designed by St. Pierre and Miquelon and typeset in Plantin. Printed by Aldgate Press

Mulberry Tree Press chronicles a fictitious publishing house created within the framework of an exhibition at the SE8 gallery in London in 2010. The exhibition included performances, discussions, and film screenings featuring 28 artists reflecting on the relationship between space, object, and text: how they exist within each other, separate from each other and side by side. The artists concerned themselves with the boundary between different states of existence, different types of production, and the translation which takes place in the passage from artist studio to gallery to printed page. One goal of the project was to turn physical artworks into a form that could work in a publication.

Plantin, a renaissance roman typeface with *"forms that aim to celebrate fine sixteenth century book typography,"* as it's described by the type foundry, is the sole typeface used throughout the book. A fitting choice for a publishing house, fictional or otherwise. The font choice gives the layout a familiar and trustworthy vibe, and the wide-legged M, open-bowled P and sturdy triangular serifs also add some friendliness to the typographic expression.

This publication falls somewhere between an exhibition catalogue and an art book. From the outset, the work it contains was meant to transition between states—from space to object to text. In some ways, any book could be said to contain aspects of these states: it can be read and reflected upon as text, it can be experienced as an object with visual and tactile characteristics, and it can even be said to be a space, with an outside and an inside, a marked entrance and various architectural properties that reveal something about its purpose. Most readers will probably remember books that have not only felt like spaces, but whole universes to enter. As a project about how different outputs reflect, interact and transform into each other, *Mulberry Tree Press* seems to encompass its focus area well—as space and experience in the past, and as book in the present.

13 March 2022

Episode 41

Die Sonne — Dreiundsechzig Holzschnitte

Written by Frans Masereel and published by Zweitausendeins in Germany in 1978

Letterpress printed and bound in laid paper

The practice of creating an image by applying ink to a matrix and pressing it onto paper was first developed in Asia (China has been cited as the origin country) and became a turning point in the democratisation of art. The relative ease and speed of printmaking made art both more widely available and more affordable to the general public. Woodcut is a style of relief printing that can be done by hand, without a printing press, a simplicity that aided its proliferation, and by the early 20th century the technique had spread across the world.

Turbulent times have historically produced strong artistic movements, and often these hands-on techniques have played an important role in activism and propaganda. The anti-war prints by artists like Käthe Kollwitz and George Grosz are famous examples, but the Belgian graphic artist Frans Masereel can certainly also be counted among political woodcut icons. Growing up, he would regularly accompany his parents to protests and from a young age he expressed contempt towards nationalism and war.

His prints focused on political and social issues and were published in many anti-war publications. During WWI he immigrated to Switzerland, but since he had refused to serve in the Belgian army he was unable to ever return to his home country. He kept contributing to Belgian publications from abroad and art became a means of participation in the political discourse, as well as in the homeland that had shut him out. During his life he published over 40 wordless graphic novels like *Le Soleil* (in German *"Die Sonne")*, both in Belgium and other countries, all while painting in Paris, teaching in Saarbrücken, or working on theatre sets in Nice.

Masereel and his printmaking contemporaries, from Mexico and the United States to Yugoslavia and the USSR, were directly responsible for making the clarity and simplicity of this handmade print aesthetic an integral part of the revolutionary visual language.

27 March 2022

Episode 42

Rab-Rab issue 4.1 and 4.2

Edited by Sezgin Boynik and published by Rab-Rab Press in Finland in 2017

Designed by Ott Kagovere and typeset in Times New Roman and L10. Printed in Estonia

"Rab-Rab" is a call ducks make in their mating ceremony, and also the independent Finnish discursive platform and publisher behind these two publications dressing up as one. Together, they make up the 4th issue of the *Journal of Political and Formal Inquiries in Art* that Rab-Rab publishes annually. Aside from the journals, which each cover a new topic (this one has the theme "Remembering as Future"), Rab-Rab's output includes artist books, pamphlets of poetry, a Soviet children's book about cinema and an anthology on the linguistic devices of Lenin.

The layout has a slight unruliness to it; type disappearing around corners, captions slanted left and right, ducks flapping around... The two-colour offset print in the first volume acts as a unifier that makes the mix of illustrations, notes, photos and other material come together as a whole. The second volume, which (aside from being Rab-Rab issue 4.2) is titled *In the Belly of the Beast: Art & Language New York Project 1972-1976,* sticks to black and white. The cover that envelops both volumes, folds out into a square poster featuring illustrations by Minna Henriksson and Michael Corris.

Times New Roman, a typeface which was commissioned for the *Times* newspaper in 1931, is the unpretentious choice for much of the body text. Despite its very print-based origin, the typeface had a big revival in the early home computer era thanks to Microsoft making it the default font in its text processor Word in 1992. It held that role for 15 years, making it a very familiar reading font for many. Its partner-in-type in this publication is a subtly playful sans serif called L10 from the Icelandic foundry Or Type. Like Times New Roman, L10 was drawn for a specific publication, in this case a book about an Icelandic art festival. Inside the covers of Rab-Rab, the two typefaces meet, each adding their own flavour to the layout.

Good Things Come in Pairs, goes the old (and worn) Chinese proverb, but not many books have this level of dualism: future and past, two books in one, two typefaces, two colours. Two Rab.

17 April 2022
Images: p. 266

Episode 43

Seth Siegelaub: Beyond Conceptual Art

Edited by Leontine Coelewij and Sara Martinetti and published by Verlag der Buchhandlung Walther König in Germany in 2016

Designed by Irma Boom and printed in the Netherlands

Previous books covered in this notes series have discussed how art can live on the printed page, and the relationship between exhibition spaces and exhibition catalogues. These issues were also very much at the heart of Seth Siegelaubs practice. During his life, Siegelaub accumulated many titles: curator, writer, art dealer, publisher, archivist, collector, bibliographer and researcher, and he's been called both the father and godfather (which sounds slightly more dramatic) of conceptual art. Born in the Bronx, he was active in the US art scene for decades, before settling in Amsterdam in the 1990s.

In 1968, Siegelaub curated *Xerox Book,* an exhibition that took the sole form of a printed volume. It was a "book-as-exhibition": a catalogue of idea-based art that was itself the primary exhibition, rather than being secondary to a physical show. Many of his projects dealt with art outside of a gallery context and the blending of mass media and high culture. More than documenting the exhibition on Siegelaub's practice, that the Stedelijk Museum opened in 2015, this publication is itself an exhibition, true to Siegelaubian form. It borrows its centred, condensed uppercase DIN cover design from the *Xerox Book*, which is one of the projects it has on display. The words on the inside of the front and back covers summarise the dualist idea: *"Catalogue as Exhibition"/"Exhibition as Catalogue"*. And the exhibition is extensive: 600 pages of 60 gsm paper, which gives it the flexible heft of a phone book, the large format and confident typography framing the material nicely. The section markings that create a diagonal dotted line along the fore-edge, as well as the edge-pushing composition on the spine, both contribute to the three-dimensional experience of the book.

Conceptual art, in some ways, offered art a liberation—from galleries, traditions, and expectations. But as its (god)father, we'd argue that Siegelaub inadvertently also helped shape conceptual publishing and our notion of what print can be.

2 May 2022
Images: p. 272

Episode 44

How to maneuver: Shapeshifting texts and other publishing tactics

Edited by Maha Maamoun and Ala Younis and co-published by Kayfa ta and Warehouse421 in the United Arab Emirates in 2021

Designed by Anton Stuckardt. Cover drawing by Hussein Nassereddine

The language(s) we speak and read are an intricate and tangled web of history, culture, references, words that mean *nearly* the same but not exactly, and words that mean *exactly* the same, but bring forth different images in the mind of different speakers, depending on their frames of reference. This entanglement of language means that any translation, no matter how thorough, will always be a little bit of a reinterpretation. A sibling of the original.

The exhibition *How to maneuver* and its accompanying publication, put focus on the different processes of publishing, the boundaries separating mainstream and independent publishing and how creative production is defined and valued. The exhibition, which opened at the end of 2019, contained books, magazines, zines, and artworks engaging with the many tactics of the publishing sphere.

Behind the project is the non-profit Arabic publishing initiative Kayfa ta, which translates to "How to". That is how all their book titles begin: *How to disappear, How to love a homeland, How to spell the fight*—the format of how-to manuals used as a tool to respond to various needs. The book was published in Arabic and English simultaneously, like fraternal twins, neither one more the original than the other, their opposite reading directions making them mirror each other. The texts are a mix of original language and translations, from English to Arabic and vice versa. The illustration on the cover shows the bookshelf (a structure surrounding publishing?), being on fire—notably not the books themselves.

"The space that separates different regimes of authorship, publishing, and readership is also the space where these differences can be negotiated," the foreword advises. Perhaps *How to maneuver* is neither an English book, nor an Arabic book, but precisely the space in between the two—not the image but the mirror itself.

23 May 2022
Images: p. 280

Episode 45

body luggage.
migration of gestures

Edited by Zasha Colah and steirischer herbst and published by Archive Books in Germany in 2016

Designed by Chiara Figone and set in Helvetica and Courier

body luggage was an exhibition shown as part of the steirischer herbst festival programme in 2016 in Graz, Austria. steirischer herbst has *"since the pivotal year of 1968"* presented an annual programme mixing visual art, music, theatre, performance, new media and literature, making it an early player within "interdisciplinary art", before that term got all but thrown around.

On the front cover, we are welcomed by Hilde Holger—an appropriate face and figure for representing "body luggage". The exhibition and publication revolve around the body's role in migration as the only constant—a container and archive of memory and experience. As philosopher Friedrich Schiller put it: *"The most secret movements of the soul are revealed on the exterior of the body."* Holger was an Austrian expressionist dancer, teacher, and choreographer who pioneered "integrated dance" and migrated more than once in her life. She was from a Jewish family and fled from Vienna when the Nazis invaded in 1939. She then lived in India until 1948 when the tension in Bombay grew and she moved to London. Inside the book we are met by an impressive collection of photographic material. The intensity and dynamism of movement, captured in stills, is the main visual voice and a three-column grid creates a calm foundation for the lively image placements. The majority of the content is printed in a warm, deep blue, creating a unified monochrome design. The book is divided into three sections, and by letting the print go to bleed in the first and using a pink paper for the last, a palette of three colours is created along the edge of the book block.

The book is set in Helvetica, appropriately placing the publication in the context of international modernism, paired with Courier, a typewriter font that leads our thoughts to archiving. A book, archiving bodies, archiving memories and experiences.

30 May 2022
Images: p. 288

Episode 46

Die Forschungsreise des Afrikaners — Lukanga Mukara ins Innerste Deutschlands

Written by Hans Paasche and published by Packpapierverlag Osnabrück in Germany ca. 1979

The German politician and writer Hans Paache was sent "to the colonies" by his father, a right wing conservative economist who had hoped to see his son follow in his footsteps, generating wealth for the Western colonisers. *"But the longer I live here, the more I see that we have to be careful with what we bring to the natives. We really think a lot of things are good that in reality have a harmful effect,"* young Paache wrote while in Africa. His years abroad made him a devout pacifist, opposed to the militaristic-nationalist Germany, advocating peace, justice, and democracy. A stance which led to his assassination by right-wing nationalists at only 39.

Forschungsreise des Afrikaners contains nine letters from the fictional Lukanga Mukara, a man conducting a research trip to Germany to observe the so-called "civil" culture, reporting back to his king with far from flattering observations. The point of the book is to flip the prevalent perspective, seeing the Western culture through the eyes of those oppressed by it. The book was first published in 1912 and this edition seems to be from 1979 (the book has no colophon). Packpapier Verlag (or *"The small publisher for big changes"*) publishes on topics from environmentalism and self-sufficiency to social movements and anarchism, and only distributes with small independent booksellers. The stapled A6 paperbacks might not last as long as a bound book would, but these books are meant to be spread and read, and their price tags of a few euros underline this focus on accessibility.

The books from Packpapier, even the newer ones, all have a playful 70s DIY vibe. Monospaced type and elegant serifs are mixed with hand lettering and various handmade illustration techniques. Different colours are used for different print sheets, or several on one, blending together in gradients and altogether hinting at a small-scale production with time and space for playful experimentations. The result is charming, each spread being a little different from the previous.

In 1912, Paache wrote: "*The suffering of the violated nature has never been as big as it is now, under the unrelenting power of world trade, traffic and industry, since the earth has existed. Wherever a protective hand can be extended over living natural treasures, it must be done now.*" A century down the line, his plea feels just as relevant. Paache's main lesson, however, might be his method of taking the perspective of the perceived 'other' and using it to take a good hard look at ourselves.

13 June 2022
Images: p. 296

Episode 47

MODES OF:
a Tin Can

Edited, designed, printed and bound by Liam Asprey, Freya Dowling, Matleena Honkanen and Tabs Portch O'Neill. Published by MODES OF in Germany in 2022

Riso-printed in an edition of 80 copies at Colorama

Spiral binds have a certain semi-professionalism to them; they require specialised equipment to put together, but with access to that, anyone can bind documents quickly and at a low cost. This accessibility, combined with traits like the ability to open flat and a spine that rotates 360 degrees, make them common for things like school workbooks, office documents and kids colouring books—practical publications with short life spans. Utility over aesthetics. But despite prosaic connotations, its qualities (aided by the wide range of colours and sizes the spirals come in) have brought spiral binding into the DIY publishing and art book scene by letting the creator bind more or less any size, page number or materials, quickly and cheaply.

MODES OF: a Tin Can matches a shiny brown plastic coil with rich, earthy card covers. Five riso colours have been used, allowing for a broad array of content styles. Using *"a range of research to facilitate new perspectives on a chosen subject matter,"* the book mixes photography, illustration, blueprint, artworks and pop-cultural appearances—ranging from the more objective and referential to interpretations and reimaginations. Each spread presents a new reading. Despite its emphasis on images, no less than four typefaces have been used in the book. Two contemporary serifs—Lust Text by American type designer Neil Summerour and Source Serif, a variable slab serif by German type whiz Frank Grießhammer—have been paired with the 1957 Max Miedinger classic Neue Haas Grotesk and Alte Haas Grotesk, a free font by French artist Yann Le Coroller, mimicking old Swiss book prints.

Like the binding, the choice of subject matter may seem mundane, but maybe there is a deeper thought exercise to attempt here. By pondering all the various shapes something can take, its potential instances, perhaps some universality can be teased out —the Platonic ideal of a tin can?

4 July 2022
Images: p. 302

Episode 48

Dear Father

Written by Dr. Balesh Jindal and published by the Writers Workshop in India in 1994

Layout and lettering by P. Lal. Hand set in Times Roman. Printed by Chakraborty Enterprise and hand stitched and hand bound by Tulamiah Mohiuddeen

Based in Kolkata, India, the Writers Workshop has been putting out English language publications since 1958. *Dear Father* is a Redbird publication, indicating it's a volume of poetry. The workshop releases many birds: "Babybird" for children's books, "Bluebird" for drama, "Silverbird" for screenplays and so on. It doesn't print well known names, it *"makes names well known, and then leaves them in the loving clutches of the so-called free market,"* the founder, Professor P. Lal, explains on the workshop's website.

Today, the Writers Workshop has put out over 3000(!) books, all from the living room of the founder, with no staff, no advertising, no budget to speak of. *"The whole process is a cottage industry style low-key entrepreneurship, in the belief that small is not only beautiful but viable as well,"* Professor Lal writes. The Writers Workshop has survived, much thanks to the founder's visits to *"hard currency lands on lecture assignments and visiting professorships, and pumping the shekels thus earned to keep alive a gasping ideal."*

The book is truly handmade: it's hand set in Times Roman and printed on a hand operated press, with calligraphy done by Professor Lal himself. The colours are vibrant, the paper bulky and pleasant to touch, and the whole thing has a sincerity to it, stemming from decades of willing books into existence through craftsmanship and devotion. Each copy is hand stitched and bound in hand woven sari fabric. The cloth is intricate, making it a challenging surface for the gold embossing, and the result is not the most sturdy cover (as the protective plastic sleeve it's sold in also implies), but—it's absolutely beautiful. Amazon lists the book as having "Unknown binding". Apparently, handmade—utterly *human made*—is not an Amazon category.

"Alternative publishing is desperately needed wherever commercial publication rules," Professor Lal writes, and we agree. Humans, with gasping ideals and able hands, are needed in a print-on-demand world.

29 August 2022

Episode 49

Funken zu Flammen — ABA AiR Berlin Alexanderplatz 10 + 1 years

Conceived and edited by Susanne Kriemann and Aleksander Komarov and published by Spector Books in Germany in 2021

Designed by Tobias Wenig and typeset in Monument Grotesk and Knif Mono

A small team of artists and researchers make up the residency initiative ABA. Their practice reflects contemporary art and research through events and salons —open-formed gatherings where participants can interact and exchange within private or public spaces that the group temporarily inhabits. *Funken zu Flammen* documents 75 of these salons, held in 48 locations over a period of 11 years.

The book is a stitched softcover and comes with several cover variations, each featuring a different composition of the letters A B A set in Monument Grotesk, a contemporary classic from the foundry ABC Dinamo. Layered on top, the title is set in the more confrontational Knif Mono, a monospace published by A is for Fonts. Its pointed serifs and terminals seem to emulate the sparks of the title and give the letters a touch of danger. Vibrant primary colours are used throughout the layout—red, yellow, blue— and looking at the photos, you get the sense that something is unusual about the print. Designer Tobias Wenig lets us in on why:

These three Pantones make up all print surfaces in the book, including the images—no black ink is used. Colours are mixed in a way that is simultaneously so familiar (it's how we learn to mix colours in kindergarten) and so unusual (you normally print with cyan, yellow, magenta, and black). This method gives the photos, taken at various times and under a variety of conditions, a unified look and gives the book a slight copier-made quality. *"The design tries to mimic a colourful telephone book or Leitz folder somehow."*

The layout balances simplicity with complexity, pure surfaces with overlaps and layering. Underpinning it all are the primary colours—pure chromatic potentials that are meeting, mixing and mingling, creating new synergies on the pages. The salons that the book describes could be said to do the same with people—create the settings for meetings, mixing and mingling. Processes where new impressions can arise.

5 September 2022
Images: p. 306

Episode 50

Notes on Book Design

Written by Siri Lee Lindskrog and Amanda-Li Kollberg (Formal Settings) and published by Onomatopee in the Netherlands in 2023

Printed on Munken Print White and Galerie Art Gloss by AS Printon in Estonia

Each of the 49 books reflected on in the preceding pages have at some point passed through Hopscotch Reading Room. Some have found their way into a tote bag or pocket and have moved on with a new owner, while others are still in the store's curated collection, waiting to be brought out, to be read on a bench, in a bar, in a bed, and then placed among new peers in a new collection. While these books *existed* at the time we wrote about them, *Notes on Book Design* did not. Content proceeds form, of course, in most book-production timelines, but this content addresses the still non-existent form that content will take—its form-to-be.

As in the case of the typefaces L10 and Times New Roman (mentioned on page 156) as well as Avant Garde (described on page 36), sometimes a typeface is occasioned by a specific project but then goes on to live independently. This book was the prompt to start drawing a text cut of Silvana, a display typeface family which we released in 2022. The body matter of the book is set with a beta version of Silvana Text, while

ABC Diatype, a sans serif released by Berlin based ABC Dinamo in 2020, acts as a supplementing typeface. In combination, the two typefaces contribute to rooting the book in its time and place of origin.

The format is 111 × 181 mm, a pocketbook size that draws a direct parallel to publishers like Albatross and Penguin Books, who from the 1930s and onward helped revolutionise the industry and pushed the democratisation of literature by making affordable and widely available books, without compromising on quality of either content or form. Many similar dimensions have been around, like the diminutive 100 × 158 mm of Reclams 1860s vending machine books and the 108 × 177 mm format of Edition Suhrkamp—books that fit effortlessly in the hand or in a pocket, ready to accompany the reader as they go about their day.

Aside from Hopscotch Reading Room and Prem Krishnamurthy, whose fore- and afterwords are the artisanal bread in this bibliophile sandwich, visual artist and regular Hopscotch goer John Seung-Hwan Lee has contributed a back cover drawing, capturing some of Hopscotch's magnetic atmosphere and the enticing mood that is characteristic of a good bookstore, library or book collection. The drawing evokes the traditional woodcuts and etchings we've come across in many older books, and adds a spatial layer to the composition—another entry point to the *Notes on Book Design* universe.

The books we've written about have undoubtedly influenced our way of working, in conscious and subconscious ways. We are keenly aware of the wealth of shoulders we stand on, the talented book designers, determined printers and passionate publishers—centuries of book-creators of all sorts. Making the heritage of book design explicit by paying a visual homage to an earlier work is something we've encountered at several points during our research for these texts. One example is Lawrence Ferlinghetti, who borrowed the cover design for a whole book series from Kenneth Patchen's *An Astonished Eye Looks Out of the Air* (as described on page 131). Another is *Tempolabor no. 3* (page 40), of which the content layout is copied from *Justine* by Marquis de Sade. It can also be said about *Seth Siegelaub — Beyond Conceptual Art* (page 160) which uses the design of one of Siegelaubs book-as-exhibitions to encompass the retrospective exhibition-as-book which was published accompanying an exhibition of his work.

Learning from, and finding inspiration in our predecessors and peers, building on techniques and tweaking ideas, are some of the biggest privileges that come with a practice that engages itself with books. This project has occasioned countless hours of interacting with and musing over books, following an almost ritualistic formula aimed at researching and reflecting on the role and potential of books, seen through a design lens. The explorative act of developing the craft is collective. The *Notes on Book Design* column has been a continuous love letter to an unparalleled medium and a singular place —both deriving their magic from the perpetual interplay between books and their people.

Visual index

MARKUS MIESSEN

9 783982 044002

14
TAGE

1. Auflage

Lektorat: Lukas Kubina
Design & Satz: Wiegand von Hartmann GbR
Druck: Druckhaus Nomos
Printed in Germany
ISBN 978-3-9820440-0-2

Mittwoch, 1. September

Das Frühstück ist geprägt von den Monologen eines Fischers (Danny), der vorschlägt, uns mit seinem long tail boat auf die andere Seite der Bucht zu fahren. Nach einer Reihe von Schnorchel-Stopps auf unbewohnten Kleinstinseln verlassen wir den Nationalpark in Richtung der Bucht von Krabi. Am Pier angekommen, realisieren wir, dass wir in der falschen Bucht sind. Das Boot ist weg. Umringt von Katzen, warten wir auf ein Zeichen. Zwei Stunden später sitzen wir in einem Toyota Hilux, Pick-Up, zweite Reihe. Ein Junge (Danny 2) bietet an, uns für 400 Baht zu chauffieren. Wir sitzen auf den perlenbesetzten Notsitzen. Farbe: Kawasaki Grün. Vor uns drei Thai Boys, die jeder vorbeilaufenden Frau auf der Straße hinterherhupen. Wir setzen nach Rai Leh über.

Donnerstag, 2. September

Der kommende Tag endet im physischen Eklat. Verschreckt von der kanarischen Resortarchitektur und den bei Long Island Ice Tea am Strand sitzenden Frankfurter Ultras, schlagen wir uns ins Hinterland. Auf dem Rückweg von einer feuchtwarmen Felshöhle, die aus unerklärbaren Gründen mit hölzernen Phallussymbolen gefüllt ist, stoßen wir auf ein Plastikschild im Gestrüpp. Es erzählt von einer Lagune. Am Rand des Schildes ist ein kleines Piktogramm abgebildet. Es zeigt einen Schuh. Der Aufstieg erscheint anfangs bequem, später kaum machbar. Die Flipflops tragen nicht zum Erfolg bei. Zweihundert Höhenmeter aufwärts realisieren wir: Eine Lagune ist ein von Meerwasser gespeister See. Es geht also wieder abwärts. Der Abstieg entpuppt sich als unmöglich. Aufgrund des Monsuns sind die Felswände

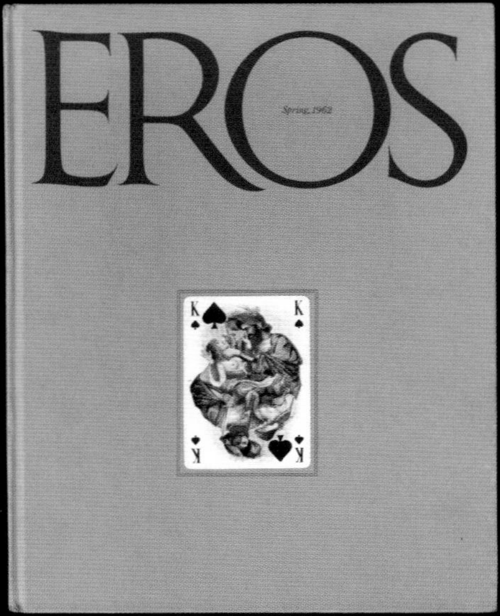
EROS
Spring, 1962

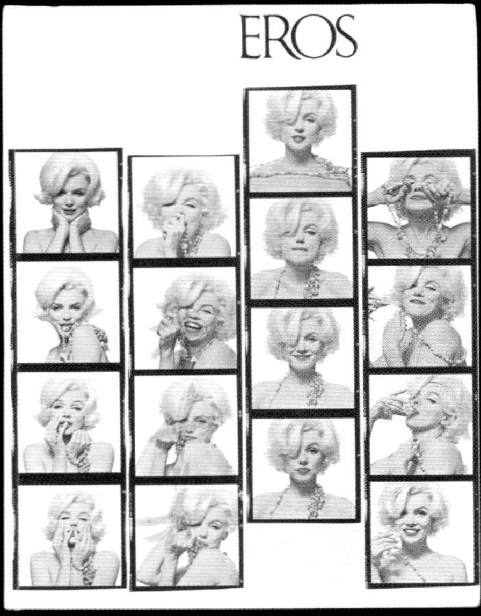
EROS

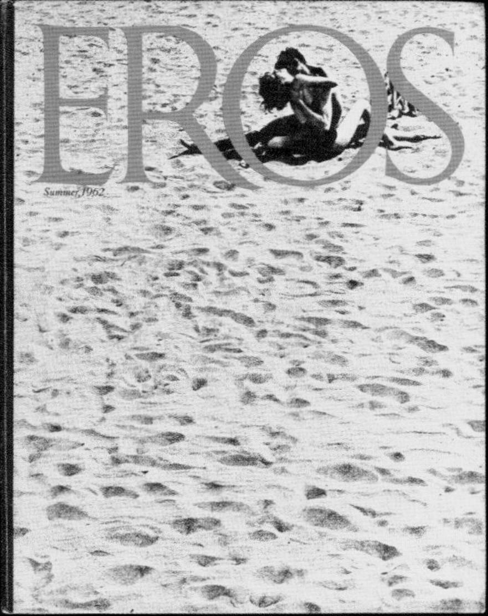
EROS
Summer, 1962

EROS
And the Lord God caused a deep
sleep to fall upon Adam....and he
took one of his ribs. Genesis 2:21
And the rib, which the Lord God
had taken from man, made he a woman, and brought her unto the man.2:22
Of every tree of the garden
thou mayest freely eat. 2:16
But of the tree of the knowledge of good and evil, thou shalt
not eat. 2:17
She took of the fruit thereof, and
did eat, and gave also unto her husband with her, and he did eat. 3:6

EROS

Summer, 1962 Volume One, Number Two

Editor And Publisher: Ralph Ginzburg
Art Director: Herb Lubalin

Associate Editors: Susan Ginzburg, David O. Wiley
Contributing Editor: Robert Knepper
Associate Publisher: Frank R. Brady
Promotion Director: John R. Nellis
Subscription Manager: Muriel Wells

Staff: Rufus Causey, Edith Colegrave, Rosemary Latimore, Tanya Moorse, Blossom Sprei Morgan, Norman Moskowitz, Roland Ray Penn, Gail Razinsky, Gerard A. Schneider, Susan Smith

"She represents to man something we all want in our unfulfilled dreams. She's the girl you'd like to double-cross your wife with." Jean Negulesco, director.

Arrival in London

Quarrel with the Protector

Apprehension by a Magistrate

Detention in Bridewell

Death

Funeral

The Clitoris

( )

A Philological Note on a Defect in Sex Organ Nomenclature

PART I

BY ABRAM BLAU, M.D.

Philology, the science that studies the structure and development of languages, has very often been invoked to assist in settling historical questions. The history of a nation's culture can be illustrated through a study of its words. This is an application of philology in a positive sense. The absence of a word, similarly, may be indicative of a widespread process of repression. The purpose of this article is to draw attention to a philological observation of significance in the psychoanalytic theory of sexuality.

The clitoris, well supplied with nerves, is the chief sexual organ in the female child and the main focus of infantile and adolescent masturbation. Only later is sexual sensation experienced in adjacent genital parts, and it is questionable whether the young female even knows about the existence of the vagina. An awareness of the clitoris as an organ must intrude upon the consciousness of the female child and adult. This must arise from the reflex erections, the spontaneous discharges of sexual excitement, pulsations and twitchings, the responses to sexual fantasies, and the reactions to local manipulations (either voluntary or by irritation of clothes and other agents). Furthermore, psychoanalytic observations offer abundant empirical evidence that the clitoris receives a great deal of attention from the female child and adult; it occupies a prominent position in the conscious sexual fantasies and is often represented symbolically in dreams.

Isn't it surprising then that, except for scientific terminology, there seems to be no vernacular, slang, or obscene word in the English or American language to designate this organ? None could be found in the Oxford New English Dictionary, Webster's New International Dictionary, Funk and Wagnalls New Standard Dictionary, the American Thesaurus of Slang by Berrey and Van den Bark, and the Dictionary of American Slang by Wentworth and Flexner. In contrast, there is no dearth of words for the male sex organ. Havelock Ellis states: "In correspondence with the importance of the penis is the large number of names which men everywhere bestowed upon it. In French literature many hundred synonyms may be found. They are also numerous in Latin. In English the literary terms for the penis seem to be comparatively few, but a large number of nonliterary synonyms exist in colloquialisms and perhaps merely local usage."

I have made inquiries among natives of other countries, psychiatrists, and lay people, and they report a similar linguistic deficiency regarding the clitoris. My inquiries have included the French, German, Spanish, Russian, Hungarian, Polish, Armenian, Turkish, Hebrew, Italian, and Arabic languages. In the German language, a synonym for clitoris does exist—Kitzler, which literally means "tickler." However, this meaningful term is not employed in the vernacular but has wholly a scientific usage. In general, the nonscientific terminology is most specific for the least sexualized genital parts, such as the uterus (womb); by contrast, only vague terms exist for the vagina. The most common slang (and obscene) references concern only the vulva in general. According to Havelock Ellis, "It is indeed but three centuries since the clitoris was so little known that (in 1559) Realdus Columbus actually claimed the honor of discovering it. Columbus was not its discoverer, for Fallopius speedily showed that Avicenna and Albucasis had referred to it."

Since this linguistic deficiency cannot be due to a true unawareness of the organ (as may be claimed regarding some internal part of the body or a nonsensitive external part), and since it is unlikely that it is the result of a linguistic laxity or insufficiency, only one conclusion is logically tenable: This imperfection in language must indicate a form of cultural evasion. Such avoidance must be significant. Ordinarily, when a sensation or emotion is common to many people, and particularly in the case of pleasurable and painful feelings, there is an impulse to interchange experiences; language generally serves this need by introducing a symbolic means of communication. The absence of a lay designation for the clitoris suggests that there is a stronger opposing influence that acts to keep it hidden and secret. Obviously, the endowment of an object with one or more names brings it a greater degree of attention and a larger means of reference. Withholding a name is equivalent to an assurance of anonymity. This is a reverse example of the power or "magic" of words and language. With a name, an object becomes a more definite part of objective reality; without one, it is obscured.

It appears to me that this lack of vocabulary cannot be attributed merely to a cultural discrimination against women regarding sex, but must have a deeper origin, arising from factors in the individual psyche. For if it were a matter of discrimination, the organ would be recognized at least in slang, or obscene wit, and there would be some reference to it among less inhibited individuals. Other ideas forbidden by moral and ethical conventions, such as masturbation and homosexuality, which have strong emotional and instinctual value, do manage to become manifest, yet these do not have even the meager cultural approbation conceded to female sexuality in the most conventional circles.

The more plausible explanation is that the language defect is due to deep individual repressions that are secondarily reflected in our culture by a deficiency in speech. The origin of the repression can be most satisfactorily understood on the basis of empirical psychoanalytic data concerning infantile sexual ideas and corresponding specific attitudes to the sex organs. An outstanding feature of these infantile notions, as Freud pointed out in his Three Contributions to the Theory of Sex, is the exaggerated evaluation of the phallus and a corresponding depreciation of its absence in the female.

The emotional counterpart of these infantile conceptions regarding the sex organs becomes evident in the individual person as penis pride, penis envy, depreciation of the female lack of the penis, and castration anxiety (concern about loss of the penis). In the face of these attitudes, the perception of the clitoris (that is, a small, inadequate, or absent penis) would excite either shame or anxiety. We would then understand this verbal ostracism of the clitoris, by both men and women, to indicate that organ as not only being unworthy of notice but as requiring special repression and concealment.

The etymology of the word clitoris is also relevant. Derived from the Greek, kleiein, meaning "to shut up," "to close," it is allied to such words as closet, clothes, cloister, closure, and so on. Webster's New International Dictionary does not consider the possibility of a psychological reason and attributes the origin of the word to the fact that the clitoris is concealed by the labia minora. Thus, the etymology of the scientific designation substantiates the notion of special seclusion, modesty, and concealment in relation to that part of the female anatomy.

In conclusion, one might contrast the unique philological exclusion of clitoris from lay language with other similar but less extensive linguistic repressions that are not uncommon—those that have adequate nomenclature, in both scientific and slang (and obscene) vocabulary, but are more or less deleted from "correct" English vernacular. They include penis, scrotum, testes, vulva, vagina, menstruation, masturbation, coitus, fellatio, pederasty, cunnilingus; feces, urine, defecation, and urination. On the other hand, some corresponding euphemistic expressions (e.g., diddle, peepee, weewee, number one, number two, to move the bowels, to pass water, to make love, and so on), obviously evasive in their very structure, do have considerable usage. Many of these vernacular expressions are employed mainly between adults and children; with the latter, evasion is more difficult and repression is as yet inadequately established.

The presumption here is that the language deficiencies are not accidental and must have some significance. Those defects that exist—such as the lack of a slang word for the clitoris—seem to highlight the extreme cultural suppression of female sexuality and the restraint on sexuality in general. In addition, they support the theory that the human being is inherently influenced by certain ideas regarding the anatomical differences between the sexes.

RASNA BHUSHAN URSULA BIEMANN PETER BRANDLMAYR CLÉMENTINE DELISS MARIANNE EIGENHEER CHARLES ESCHE EWA ESTERHAZY JEAN-PAUL FELLEY IZETA GRADEVIC ERIC HATTAN HELEN HIRSCH RUMMANA HUSSAIN OLIVIER KAESER BIRGIT KEMPKER JÖRG LENZLINGER RENÉE LEVI VIA LEWANDOWSKY HEINRICH LÜBER MUDA MATHIS CLAUDIA MÜLLER JULIA MÜLLER MARIANNE MÜLLER TIM NEUGER OLAF NICOLAI PETER PAKESCH DAN PETERMAN MARIA PISTOLETTO MICHELANGELO PISTOLETTO STEPHEN PRINA MARTIN PRINZHORN PROGETTO ARTE TOBIAS REHBERGER LEILA SADEGHEE ISSA SAMB NICOLAUS SCHAFHAUSEN MADELEINE SCHUPPLI ANDREW SHIELDS KAN-SI MARTINA SIEGWOLF GERDA STEINER REINHARD STORZ PETER SUTER WAWRZYNIEC TOKARSKI ANNETTE UNGAR ANDREA SILVIA VÉGH CYRIL VERRIER NEBOJSA VILIC SUS ZWICK

KUNSTHALLE BASEL
SCHWABE & CO. AG

METRONOME No. 3

TEMPOLABOR

A LIBERTINE LABORATORY?

Edited by
CLÉMENTINE DELISS

Basel 1998

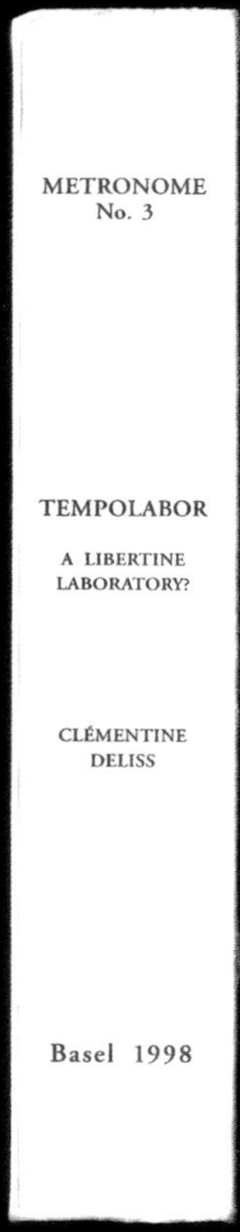
METRONOME
No. 3
TEMPOLABOR
A LIBERTINE
LABORATORY?
CLÉMENTINE
DELISS
Basel 1998

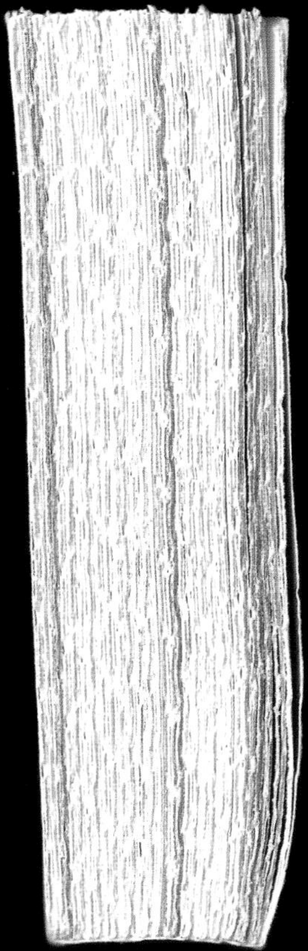

"imaginary politic" or an "abstract politic". *(silence)* I use the term "lived experience", for instance, instead of talking about "reality". It's closer to what I would want to describe. I would never approach the description of processes within art as being connected to the "real" or not. What happens in a museum would be conceivably as real as what happens outside of it.

Clémentine Deliss: That's a healthy remark! It's bound to happen that we face terminological discrepancies.

Dan Peterman: Something that does come to mind is what happens on the internet when discussions are going on. Things get framed, just like Stephen framed his comment as an off-topic, not directly related to what I've been saying. Actually this is very useful and people should feel free to make off-comments.

Stephen Prina: I have a different kind of aside. It's not about a particular example used in the Tempolabor so far. But let's say that I was involved in Lacanian analysis. I am not a Lacanian, but for reasons particular to Lacanian psychoanalysis, you have the symbolic and you have the imaginary and you have the real. The real is that to which we have no access. We only have access to the symbolic things of the world that we can actually work on. The real is out of our reach. The real is by definition inaccessible. That is an example which I think could turn some of the discussions on their head. That's why it is very important to keep those distinctions.

Issa Samb: Stephen, je pense que ce que Dan nous a pas dit, c'est le risque qu'il a été obligé de prendre, et qu'il est

obligé de continuer de prendre. Mais en tenant bien sûr compte du fait que, quelque part, nous sommes un peu éloignés de la réalité. Mais, cette réalité-là, est-ce qu'elle va sans la responsabilité que celle que Dan a prise?

Stephen Prina: I don't think I understand.

Clémentine Deliss (addressing Issa): Stephen a dit qu'il préfère parler d'expérience vécue. Parce qu'il n'y a pas de distinction entre une réalité d'un côté et la représentation d'une réalité de l'autre. Il y a des problèmes avec les mots, une distinction qui apparaît de temps en temps …

Issa Samb: Je pense que ce qui se passe, c'est que lui, Dan, vit au coeur de la réalité, et il assume des responsabilités. Maintenant, est-ce qu'il n'est pas en danger en tant que créateur, dans une ville comme Chicago?

Clémentine Deliss: Nous nous trouvons dans une situation inter-disciplinaire et inter-culturelle, inter-terminologique et inter-temporaire.

Scene IV

(Nebojsa Vilic prepares to give his talk. Everyone remains in the boudoir, seated closely together. Leila Sadeghee offers massages to those with bad backs.)

Nebojsa Vilic: I'd like to make a comment on the question of reality. Stephen, do you make a distinction between an art reality and an objective reality?

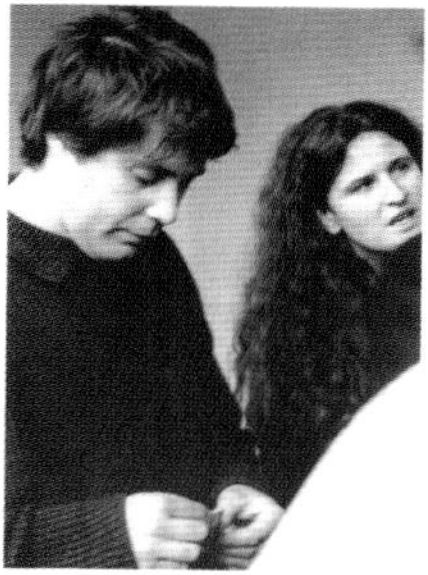

fig. 77

fig. 78

the kinds of instruments you build up to survive, physically and psychologically, that interested us. How, for example, did one go about protecting oneself? I don't think this was so particular to Sarajevo. It happens everywhere, world-wide. For example, in the poor areas of big cities in the United States, I saw, written on children's faces, the same kind of awareness of possible danger that I'd seen on kids in Sarajevo for a long time. They build up small antennae to keep alert. Maybe the next step they take will be very dangerous and someone will come around the corner. It's a similiar type of fear, only what we had in Sarajevo was somehow much more compressed.

We built up tools for survival, very small things. For example, we charged up our batteries through the telephone. We'd make a small charger, disconnect the receiver and put this gadget on the phone overnight. The town had very few lines and because ten of us were living in an empty house, they gave us one. That way you could call if there was a fire, or if someone was dead or wounded. Starting from that small gadget and building right up to a gallery event was extraordinary. Occasionally, people would cry when they saw the art works.

Peter Pakesch: Could you describe in what direction the Obala Center and your thinking are heading at the moment?

Izeta Gradevic: I'm a little tired of all the troubles. It's physically very exhausting. I'll stop running the gallery soon and try and find a fresh and enthusiastic person to take over. Obala also has a small cinema and we are trying to put together a good programme. We're not trying to be

st 556
Kerr (Hrsg.) Über Robert Walser 3
st 1638
Barnes Ryder
st 1541
Juan Goytisolo Johann ohne Land
st w 1722
Hegel Philosophie der Kunst (1826)
st 1371
Abish Das ist kein Zufall

Ludmilla trägt ein purpurfarbenes Kleid, das ihren Rücken fast ganz dem Blick freigibt. Ich zeichne ihr die Buchstaben L.O.V.E. auf den Rücken, aber sie unterläßt es, zu reagieren. Sie ist keine, mit der man tändelt. Liebe, so grüble ich, ist ganz und gar entbehrlich geworden.
st
ISBN 3-518-37871-6
Walter Abish
Das ist kein Zufall
suhrkamp taschenbuch

Wir finden, daß die Kunst eine Art und Weise ist, wie dem Menschen zum Bewußtsein gebracht ist, was das höchste Interesse seines Geistes ist. Die Kunst enthält den Schlüssel von der Weisheit bei vielen Nationen ausschließlich.

stw

Originalausg

ISBN 3-518-2932

9 783518 2932

10,00 [D]

Georg Wilhelm Friedrich Hegel
Philosophie der Kunst

Vorlesung von 1826

suhrkamp taschenbuch wissenschaft

Mit Beiträgen von:
John Christopher Middleton
Marthe Robert
Aloisio Rendi
George C. Avery
Walter Weideli
Roberto Calasso
Vladimir Sedelnik
Renata Buzzo Màrgari
Tudor Olteanu
Domingo Pérez-Minik
Claudio Magris
Marian Holona
François Bondy
Giovanni Mariotti
Giovanni Orelli

st

ISBN 3-518-37056-

Über Robert Walser

Dritter Band

Herausgegeben von
Katharina Kerr

suhrkamp
taschenbuch

suhrkamp taschenbuch 556

Walter Abish, geboren 1931 in Wien, lebt in New York.

In Walter Abishs zwölf zusammenhängenden Erzählungen wird der Leser auf eine Wanderung zwischen den Welten geschickt: da ist einerseits der vertraute Alltag mit seinen Individuen, welchen das Abweichen vom Durchschnitt Mühe bereitet; andererseits sind Alltag wie Durchschnitt bereits genau vermessen, und die Geschehnisse scheinen sich in einem neuen, uns fremden Maßstab abzuspielen, noch kenntlich zwar und offenbar höchst präzise, aber mit beträchtlicher Verzerrung.

Abish hat sich auf seinen Erkundungen der technisch fortgeschrittenen und maschinell verletzten menschlichen Gefühlswelt sein europäisches Erbe bewahrt.

Es besteht im Stellen von Fragen, die das Geschilderte mit einem ebenso kritischen wie fantastischen Netz überziehen. Warum sollen zwei Brüder unter Napoleon Signaltürme konstruieren? Ist es bekannt, daß Geraldine einen Anruf von Mr. Frank Ol erhielt? Wird Bill den Standort für seine Stadt richtig auswählen? Toleriert Ludmilla mein pflichtvergessenes Sexualverhalten? Was hat Marcel Proust mit den Taxifahrern in Albuquerque zu schaffen? Abishs Eigentümlichkeit besteht darin, daß diese Fragen eher auf neue Tatbestände verweisen als zu raschen Antworten verleiten. Er wird seinem Ruf gerecht, Amerikas raffiniertester Beitrag zu Österreichs Hintersinn zu sein.

Walter Abish
Das ist kein Zufall

Erzählungen

Suhrkamp

George C. Avery

Zum dritten Berliner Roman Robert Walsers: *Jakob von Gunten*

Eine grundlegende Prämisse dieser Studie[1] ist die Modernität von Walsers Werk, oder genauer, die Modernität der Grundzüge, welche seine Romane mit dem europäischen Roman, wie er sich im ersten Drittel dieses Jahrhunderts entwickelte, gemeinsam haben. Diese Prämisse könnte man jedoch mit Recht in Frage stellen, hat doch Walser selbst nie irgendein Interesse an engagiert moderner Literatur bekundet, auch nicht als Anhänger einer besonderen literarischen Bewegung verstanden sein wollen und, soweit bekannt ist, außer dem Frühwerk von Thomas Mann und Hugo von Hofmannsthal die Werke seiner Zeitgenossen weder gelobt noch bewundert. Die wenigen Schweizer Literaturkritiker, welche sich mit Walser beschäftigten und deren Interesse über bloßen Lokalpatriotismus hinausging, haben diese Frage nicht gestellt. Statt dessen waren sie mehr daran interessiert, die Grenzen von Walsers künstlerischer Bedeutung gegenüber der impliziten Annahme zu definieren, daß der Preis politischer Freiheit eine auf praktische Realitäten reagierende, ethisch konformistische Gesellschaft sei. Der offenkundigste Ausdruck von Walsers Modernität, nämlich seine Konzentration auf das Bewußtsein einzelner Protagonisten, liegt seinem ganzen Werk zugrunde, angefangen bei den frühen kurzen Versdramoletten, bei den Romanen, Prosastücken, den Dialogen und sogenannten Essays aus der letzten Phase seines Schaffens. In dieser Optik liegt Walsers Antwort auf die Rolle des Menschen in der modernen Gesellschaft; sie zeigt sich auch im Zusammenhang der zentralen Metaphern in seinem Werk und objektiviert und verwandelt Walsers ständige Beschäftigung mit einer offensichtlich autobiographischen persona in paradigmatische Kunst. Das Schweizer Erbe Walsers, erkennbar in der Art der Darstellung und literarischen Formung menschlicher Erfahrung, erweist sich damit als Teil einer wesensmäßig europäischen Tradition – und dies ist ein verpflichtenderes und tieferes Bekenntnis zu seiner Heimat als es mit konventionellen

Schlagwörtern zu leisten wäre: es liegt darin das Wissen um die Notwendigkeit, Veränderbarkeit als Voraussetzung humanen Verständnisses und Fortschritts zu akzeptieren. Walser gibt seiner poetischen Vision eine moderne ästhetische Formulierung als Wechselwirkung zwischen absoluter Subjektivität und ihrer metaphorischen Funktion. Ein neues Bewußtsein der Vielfalt menschlicher Erscheinungen wird erst aus diesem Wissen möglich, und nicht aus der Unterwürfigkeit gegenüber Institutionen oder aus der Verteidigung von Systemen.

Walsers Modernität ist auch in seinem anti-ästhetischen schöpferischen Ethos erkennbar, das sein ganzes Werk in verschiedenen Erscheinungsformen durchzieht und das stets von starker Sensibilität und künstlerischem Können getragen ist. In der Dichotomie dieser Gegenläufigkeit liegt Walsers Bedeutung für das moderne Temperament. Indem er eine in Bruchstücken gezeichnete kreative Persönlichkeit als Symbol des dynamischen Kontinuums wählt, legt Walsers Schaffen – durch das Medium der Kunst selbst – eine ambivalente Haltung gegenüber der Funktion und Wirksamkeit der Wortkunst bloß, welche er mit so andersartigen Zeitgenossen wie Franz Kafka, Thomas Mann und Bertolt Brecht teilte. Was Walser von diesen Autoren unterscheidet, ist seine augenfällige Nichtbeachtung der Tradition der Literaturgattungen, in welchen er schrieb. Während es keinen Beweis gibt, nach dem man Walser in die Gruppe der bewußt Experimentierenden in der deutschen Literatur nach 1900 einreihen müßte, und während sein Umgang mit der Kunst ein Zeichen seiner Überzeugung von der Gleichwertigkeit der literarischen Gattungen ist, nehmen seine Romane – vor allem was ihren ästhetischen Nutzen und ihre metaphorische Aussage angeht – das Raffinement voraus, welches in der Erscheinung tiefer Aussagen im Gewand der unprätentiösen Form liegt und welches dann besonders in der kurzen Prosa zu finden sein wird. Auch hier wird die Vorrangigkeit der persönlichen, antitraditionellen literarischen Sprache betont.

Die zentralen Gestalten in Walsers Romanen werden in dieser Studie deshalb als Helden bezeichnet, weil Walser für sie die in der modernen Literatur einzig glaubhafte Art anwendet, heldenmäßige Figuren zu schildern: Gestalten, welche sich resolut dagegen zur Wehr setzen, etwas anderes oder mehr zu sein, als sie tatsächlich sind. Diese Helden haben aber mit ihren heutigen

209

ALS MUREN OREN HADDEN
IF WALLS HAD EARS

RECENTE BEELDENDE KUNSTONTWIKKELINGEN
IN EEN INTERNATIONAAL PERSPECTIEF

KRITISCHE VISIES OP RECENTE ONTWIKKELINGEN IN DE BEELDENDE KUNST: OVER INDIVIDUELE OBSESSIES, MAATSCHAPPELIJK ENGAGEMENT, INSTALLATIEKUNST, KUNSTHALLEN, PERFORMANCES EN PUBLIEKSPARTICIPATIE, PUBLICATIES, MICRO- EN MACROWERELDEN, DE ROL VAN DE CURATOR EN KUNST ALS VRIJPLAATS

OVERZICHT ACTIVITEITEN EN TENTOONSTELLINGEN
DE APPEL 1984–2005

RECENT ART DEVELOPMENTS IN
AN INTERNATIONAL PERSPECTIVE

CRITICAL VIEWS ON RECENT DEVELOPMENTS IN ART: ON INDIVIDUAL OBSESSIONS, SOCIAL ENGAGEMENT, INSTALLATION ART, ART CENTRES, PERFORMANCES AND AUDIENCE PARTICIPATION, PUBLICATIONS, MICRO AND MACRO WORLDS, THE ROLE OF THE CURATOR AND ART AS A SPACE OF FREEDOM

SURVEY OF ACTIVITIES AND EXHIBITIONS
DE APPEL 1984–2005

REDACTIE
EDITED BY

EDNA VAN DUYN

MET TEKSTEN VAN
WITH TEXTS BY

MICHAEL ARCHER
SASKIA BOS
CHARLES ESCHE
EDNA VAN DUYN
HOU HANRU
JORG HEISER
GAVIN JANTJES
LUK LAMBRECHT
ANNELIE POHLEN

ISBN 90-73501-66-0
9 789073 501669

ALS MUREN OREN HADDEN
DE APPEL
AMSTERDAM

WALL

(front to back)
Matthew McCaslin
Trident, 1985
Mark Stahl
Chain Gang, 1987
Christian Eckard
Illumination Gray, 1987

Peter Hopkins (left)
It's a small world, 1987
Alive with pleasure, 1987

Wallace & Donohue (right)
Fucking as the public mind, 1987

The art of the real, 1987

Fabrice Hybert
Pof no. 65, ballon carré, 1998

Fabrice Hybert
Pof no. 16, pant-chaise, 1998

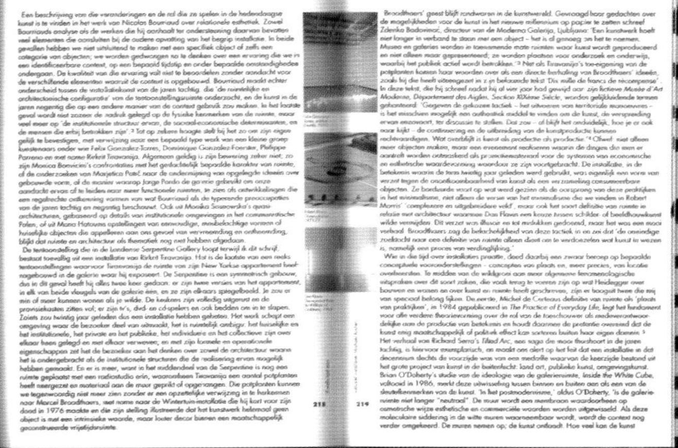

Een beschrijving van die veranderingen en de rol die ze spelen in de hedendaagse kunst is te vinden in het werk van Nicolas Bourriaud over *relationele esthetiek*. Zowel Bourriauds analyse als de werken die hij aanhaalt ter ondersteuning daarvan bevatten veel elementen die aansluiten bij de oudere opvatting van het begrip installatie. In beide gevallen hebben we niet uitsluitend te maken met een specifiek object of zelfs een categorie van objecten; we worden gedwongen na te denken over een ervaring die we in een identificeerbare context, op een bepaald tijdstip en onder bepaalde omstandigheden ondergaan. De kwaliteit van die ervaring valt niet te beoordelen zonder aandacht voor de verschillende elementen waaruit de context is opgebouwd. Bourriaud maakt echter onderscheid tussen de installatiekunst van de jaren tachtig, die 'de ruimtelijke en architectonische configuratie' van de tentoonstellingsruimte onderzocht, en de kunst in de jaren negentig die op een andere manier van de context gebruik zou maken. In het laatste geval wordt niet zozeer de nadruk gelegd op de fysieke kenmerken van de ruimte, maar veel meer op 'de institutionele structuur ervan, de sociaal-economische determinanten, en de mensen die erbij betrokken zijn'.[2] Tot op zekere hoogte stelt hij het zo om zijn eigen gelijk te bevestigen, met verwijzing naar een bepaald type werk van een kleine groep kunstenaars onder wie Felix Gonzalez-Torres, Dominique Gonzalez-Foerster, Philippe Parreno en met name Rirkrit Tiravanija. Algemeen geldig is zijn bewering zeker niet; zo zijn Monica Bonvicini's confrontaties met het gendachtelijk bepaalde karakter van ruimte, of de onderzoeken van Marjetica Potrč naar de ondermijning van opgelegde ideeën over gebouwde vorm, of de manier waarop Jorge Pardo de galerie gebruikt om onze aandacht ervan af te leiden naar meer functionele ruimten, te zien als ontwikkelingen die een regelrechte ontkenning vormen van wat Bourriaud als de typerende preoccupaties van de jaren tachtig en negentig beschouwt. Ook uit Monika Sosnowska's quasi-architecturen, gebaseerd op details van institutionele omgevingen in het communistische Polen, of uit Mona Hatoums opstellingen van eenvoudige, meubelachtige vormen of huiselijke objecten die appelleren aan ons gevoel van vervreemding en ontheemding, blijkt dat ruimte en architectuur als thematiek nog niet hebben afgedaan.

De tentoonstelling die in de Londense Serpentine Gallery loopt terwijl ik dit schrijf, bestaat toevallig uit een installatie van Rirkrit Tiravanija. Het is de laatste van een reeks tentoonstellingen waarvoor Tiravanija de ruimte van zijn New Yorkse appartement heeft nagebouwd in de galerie waar hij exposeert. De Serpentine is een symmetrisch gebouw, dus in dit geval heeft hij alles twee keer gedaan: er zijn twee versies van het appartement, in elk van beide vleugels van de galerie één, en ze zijn elkaars spiegelbeeld. Je zou er min of meer kunnen wonen als je wilde. De keukens zijn volledig uitgerust en de provisiekasten zitten vol; er zijn tv's, dvd- en cd-spelers en ook bedden om in te slapen. Zoiets zou twintig jaar geleden dus een installatie hebben geheten. Het werk schept een omgeving waar de bezoeker deel van uitmaakt, het is ruimtelijk ambigu: het huiselijke en het institutionele, het private en het publieke, het individuele en het collectieve zijn over elkaar heen gelegd en met elkaar verweven; en met zijn formele en operationele eigenschappen zet het de bezoeker aan het denken over zowel de architectuur waarin het is ondergebracht als de institutionele structuren die de realisering ervan mogelijk hebben gemaakt. En er is meer, want in het middendeel van de Serpentine is nog een ruimte geplaatst met een radiostudio erin, waaromheen Tiravanija een aantal potplanten heeft neergezet en materiaal aan de muur geprikt of opgehangen. Die potplanten kunnen we tegenwoordig niet meer zien zonder er een opzettelijke verwijzing in te herkennen naar Marcel Broodthaers, met name naar de Wintertuin-installatie die hij kort voor zijn dood in 1976 maakte en die zijn stelling illustreerde dat het kunstwerk helemaal geen object is met een intrinsieke waarde, maar louter decor binnen een maatschappelijk geconstrueerde vrijetijdsruimte.

218

219

Broodthaers' geest blijft rondwaren in de kunstwereld. Gevraagd haar gedachten over de mogelijkheden voor de kunst in het nieuwe millennium op papier te zetten schreef Zdenka Badovinac, directeur van de Moderna Galerija, Ljubljana: 'Een kunstwerk hoeft niet langer in verband te staan met een object – het is al genoeg om het te noemen. Musea en galeries worden in toenemende mate ruimten waar kunst wordt geproduceerd en niet alleen maar gepresenteerd; ze worden plaatsen voor onderzoek en onderwijs, waarbij het publiek actief wordt betrokken.'[3] Niet als Tiravanija's toe-eigening van de potplanten komen haar woorden over als een directe herhaling van Broodthaers' ideeën, zoals hij die heeft uiteengezet in zijn bekende tekst 'Dix mille de francs de récompense'. In deze tekst, die hij schreef nadat hij al vier jaar had gewijd aan zijn fictieve *Musée d'Art Moderne, Département des Aigles, Section XIXème Siècle*, worden gelijkluidende termen gehanteerd: 'Gegeven de gekozen tactiek – het uitvoeren van territoriale manoeuvres – is het misschien mogelijk een authentiek middel te vinden om de kunst, de verspreiding ervan enzovoort, ter discussie te stellen. Dat zou – of blijft het onduidelijk, hoe je er ook naar kijkt – de continuering en de uitbreiding van de kunstproductie kunnen rechtvaardigen. Wat overblijft is kunst als productie als productie.'[4] Ofwel: niet alleen meer objecten maken, maar een evenement realiseren waarin de dingen die men er aantreft worden ontmaskerd als promotiemateriaal voor de systemen van economische en esthetische waardevorming waardoor ze zijn voortgebracht. De installatie, in de betekenis waarin de term twintig jaar geleden werd gebruikt, was eigenlijk een vorm van verzet tegen de onontkoombaarheid van kunst als een verzameling consumeerbare objecten. Ze borduurde voort op wat werd gezien als de oorsprong van deze praktijken in het minimalisme, niet alleen de versie van het minimalisme die we vinden in Robert Morris' 'complexere en uitgebreidere veld', maar ook het soort definitie van ruimte in relatie met architectuur waarmee Dan Flavin een keuze tussen schilder- of beeldhouwkunst wilde vermijden. Dit verzet was illusoir en tot mislukken gedoemd, maar het was een mooi verhaal. Broodthaers zag de belachelijkheid van deze tactiek in en zei dat 'de oneindige zoektocht naar een definitie van ruimte alleen dient om te verdoezelen wat kunst in wezen is, namelijk een proces van verdinglijking.'

Wie in die tijd over installaties praatte, deed daarbij een zwaar beroep op bepaalde conceptuele vooronderstellingen – concepten van plaats en, meer precies, van locatie overheersten. Te midden van de wildgroei aan meer algemene fenomenologische uitspraken over dit soort zaken, die vaak terug te voeren zijn op wat Heidegger over bouwen en wonen en over kunst en ruimte heeft geschreven, zijn er hooguit twee die mij van speciaal belang lijken. De eerste, Michel de Certeaus definitie van ruimte als 'plaats van praktijken', in 1984 gepubliceerd in *The Practice of Everyday Life*, legt het fundament voor alle verdere theorievorming over de rol van de toeschouwer als medeverantwoordelijke aan de productie van betekenis en houdt daarmee de pretentie overeind dat de kunst enig maatschappelijk of politiek effect kan sorteren buiten haar eigen domein.[5] Het verhaal van Richard Serra's *Tilted Arc*, een saga die maar doorsleept in de jaren tachtig, is hiervoor exemplarisch, en maakt ons alert op het feit dat een installatie in dat decennium slechts de voorzijde was van een medaille waarvan de keerzijde bestond uit het grote project van kunst in de buitenlucht: land art, publieke kunst, omgevingskunst. Brian O'Doherty's studie van de ideologie van de galerieruimte, *Inside the White Cube*, voltooid in 1986, merkt deze uitwisseling tussen binnen en buiten aan als een van de sleutelkenmerken van de kunst. 'In het postmodernisme,' aldus O'Doherty, 'is de galerieruimte niet langer "neutraal". De muur wordt een membraan waardoorheen op osmotische wijze esthetische en commerciële waarden worden uitgewisseld. Als deze moleculaire siddering in de witte muren waarneembaar wordt, wordt de context nog verder omgekeerd. De muren nemen op; de kunst ontlaadt. Hoe veel kan de kunst

Carlos Amorales
Notions of advanced fighting, 2000

Tariq Alvi
untitled, 2000

Extra Volume

THE · ALBATROSS · LIBRARY
THE · ALBATROSS · MODERN · CONTINENTAL · LIBRARY
VICTORIA OF ENGLAND
by
EDITH SITWELL
THE ALBATROSS
COPYRIGHT EDITION
NOT TO BE INTRODUCED INTO THE BRITISH EMPIRE OR THE U. S. A.
HAMBURG · PARIS · BOLOGNA

21

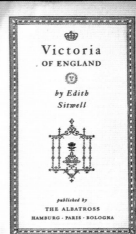

Victoria
OF ENGLAND

by Edith Sitwell

published by
THE ALBATROSS
HAMBURG · PARIS · BOLOGNA

sting me to the heart. God help you and your affairs.' And Albert made it quite clear that *he* would not. The heart, indeed, however stung, remained singularly untouched, although Albert had a large allowance, was married to the Queen of England, whilst his brother was poor. But then we must remember that Prince Ernest had offended against Albert's sense of morality. I do not know in what, exactly, the offence consisted, but he had undoubtedly been involved in some scandal, his health was affected, and Prince Albert in a letter that seems strangely cruel, coming as it did from a man whose heart was warm and compassionate, told him that, though he would never curse him or take away the love he owed him as a brother, he found it necessary to 'leave him to perish in immorality'. Nor, he added, could he allow Prince Ernest to visit England at present. The invitation sent he regarded as cancelled. 'Nothing,' he added, 'would be more disagreeable at present than your visit.' The only thing left for Prince Ernest to do—and this was made plain—was for him to marry a virtuous wife—in which case he would be put right in the eyes of the world, and his misdemeanours would be forgotten.

In a short time Prince Ernest married Princess Alexandrina of Baden, and his brother and sister-in-law, forgetting the requests for money, and the necessity of leaving him to perish in immorality, invited him to spend his honeymoon at Claremont.

CHAPTER FIFTEEN

VISITS AND VISITORS

THE YEAR 1844 BEGAN SADLY ENOUGH; FOR DUKE Ernest, whose principles, some time before, had cut Prince Albert to the heart, died in January, and the Queen, who had met him for a short while in 1836, and again at the time of the marriage, was dissolved in tears. She was, she assured the King of the Belgians, crushed, overwhelmed, bowed down, and to describe to her dearly beloved uncle, who must now be the father to those two broken-hearted bereaved children, herself and her husband, all that the children in question had suffered, would be difficult. The violence of their grief might be over; but, she added, the desolation which now invaded them was worse, and tears were undoubtedly a relief.

As for the Duke's younger son, writing to the new Duke Ernest, who so lately had been in such deep disgrace, he exclaimed: 'We have no home any more, and this is a terrible idea. . . . I am far away from you, but the whole love of a brother fills my heart, and I shall always stand by you with advice and deed. . . . Our poor little children do not know why we cry, and they ask us why we are in black.

'. . . Victoria weeps with me, for me, and for all of you. This is a great comfort for me, and your dear Alexandrina will weep with you. Let us take great care of these two jewels; let us love and protect them, as in them we shall find happiness again. . . . Victoria . . . sends you a pin with a curl of dear Father's hair.'[1]

Still worse was to come, for Prince Albert must go to

[1] Bolitho, *op. cit.*, p. 127.

THIS EDITION IS COMPOSED IN BASKERVILLE TYPE CUT BY THE MONOTYPE CORPORATION. THE PAPER IS MADE BY THE BAUTZEN PAPERMILL. THE PRINTING AND THE BINDING OF THIS SECOND IMPRESSION ARE THE WORK OF OSCAR BRANDSTETTER LEIPZIG

Michel Leiris
Die Spielregel
1
Streichungen
Matthes & Se
Michel Leiris
Die Spielregel
2
Krempel
Matthes & Seitz

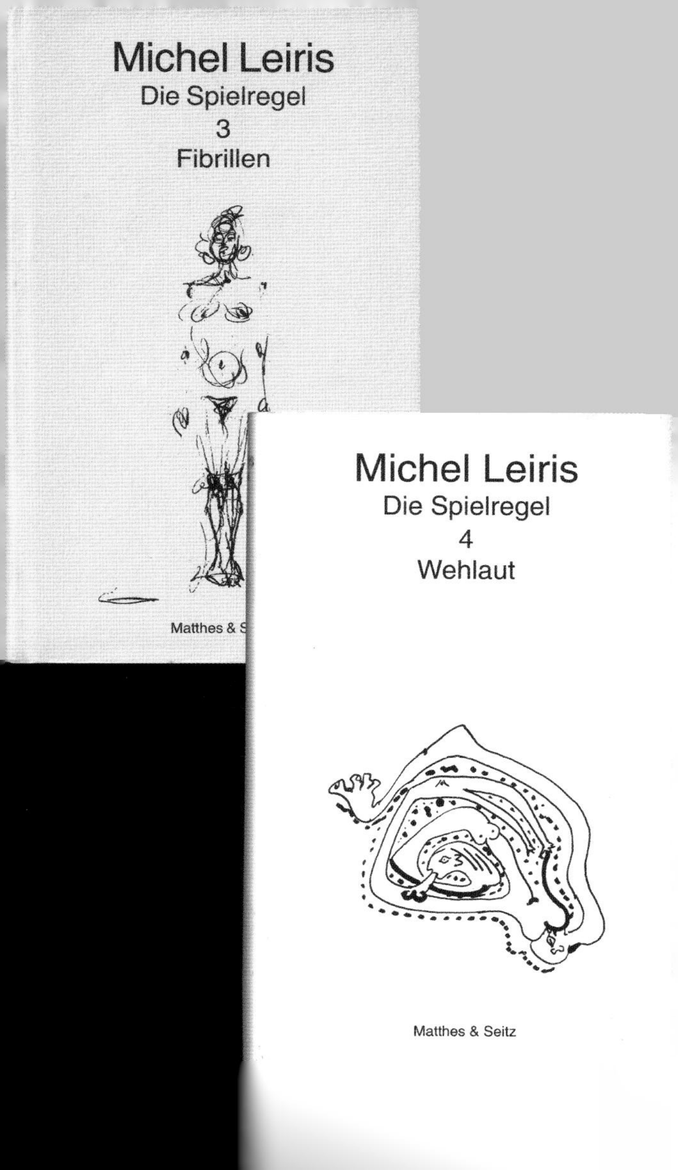
Michel Leiris
Die Spielregel
3
Fibrillen
Matthes &
Michel Leiris
Die Spielregel
4
Wehlaut
Matthes & Seitz

Michel Leiris
Die Spielregel
1
Streichungen
Michel Leiris
Die Spielregel
2
Krempel
Michel Leiris
Die Spielregel
3
Fibrillen
Michel Leiris
Die Spielregel
4
Wehlaut

Gisèle Freund: Michel Leiris, 1966

Michel Leiris

Die Spielregel
Band 3

Fibrillen

Aus dem Französischen
von Hans Therre

Mit einem Essay
von László F. Földényi

Matthes & Seitz Verlag
München

24

Every few thousand years, the North and South poles flip in an epic act of geomagnetic gymnastics. Such reversals and readjustments are inscribed onto our epigenetic archive: we find ways to walk on our heads so things don't seem as upside d o w n .

The poles do what they want. They make wild transitions: tropical paradises that age into frigid neverlands. Astronomer by day, astrologer by night. While cartographers fashioned the middle latitudes into being, these monstrous otherlands went unmapped. They were Uranian: the anti-human, the negative space that contained the non-world.

Queerity is vulnerability.

The poles became the target of the temperate w o r l d ' s machinery and are now places that experience severe loss.

In Antarctica, whole ice shelves the size of countries have broken off: a traumatised body. The Arctic's glaciers are receding: disembodied land. Like any marginalized entity foraging for a future, their emancipatory rituals inspire fantasies of freedom. In this eccentric embodiment of alienness, they open themselves up to the wild imaginaries of hybrid morphologies that more normative societies can not a c c e p t .

When Pytheas went on a circumpolar voyage in 350 BCE, he found the mythical Thule, a place beyond the north star on the celestial map of his time. In 330 BCE, in *Meteorology*, Aristotle hypothesised that a mythic southern continent must exist, based simply on the belief in a fundamental equilibrium. He named Antarctica from the Greek anti and arks, meaning 'opposite the bear', the name for the constellation under which the Arctic lay.

(The division of BCE and AD are as polarizing as the temporalities of Antarctica before and after it was discovered: once a flag had been placed on it, it became part of the teleological world).

Cicero's 50 BCE theory of mirroring hemispheres is one in which the earth is bookended by ice, with an incinerating heat at its belly. If the South was the exact opposite of the North, then perhaps people in the South walked backwards. This idea is the basis of the etymology of the words antipodes (opposite feet) and antichthon (counter world). The sun rose in the west and set in the east. If the north was cold, the south was hot. If the North was civilized, the South was savage.

The poles resent this dyadic thinking, protesting that they aren't irrelevant 'there's, but manifestations of repressed 'here's.

Over time, Antarctica became home to the freaks of the male, medieval geographer's imagination. In the Hereford map, drawn by Richard of Holdingham in the 1280's, Antarctica is infested with mythical beasts such as Blemyae, with eyes and mouths on their breasts,

THINKING LIKE AN ISLAND.

We think like an island.
We are both our bodies and the
water that
we resist.

We
We
We are made from an explosion
and also an erosion.

We are delusional.
W
wwwwwwwwwwwwwwwwwwwwwww we die and
every time,

up for a little more clarity.
e
s
i
our souls r We
wake up to take the
oblique journey
back to the shore.
We
We
We
We
We are
deserted in the world's noisy grief
and still,
w e are the stillness.
We are briefly
the bomb
in Baghdad.
We are
the finite area and
the infinite perimeter.

opposite
We are like that

A half-life
of love mixed with time running out,
trying always
to give it word
so it stays —
s s s
Trying always to stay —

far
enough
from its
radiation
so it never withers
like the
c
o
rner stone of Kaaba is wither-
ing
from the multitude of
kisses lain upon it.

James Baldwin Giovannis Zimmer

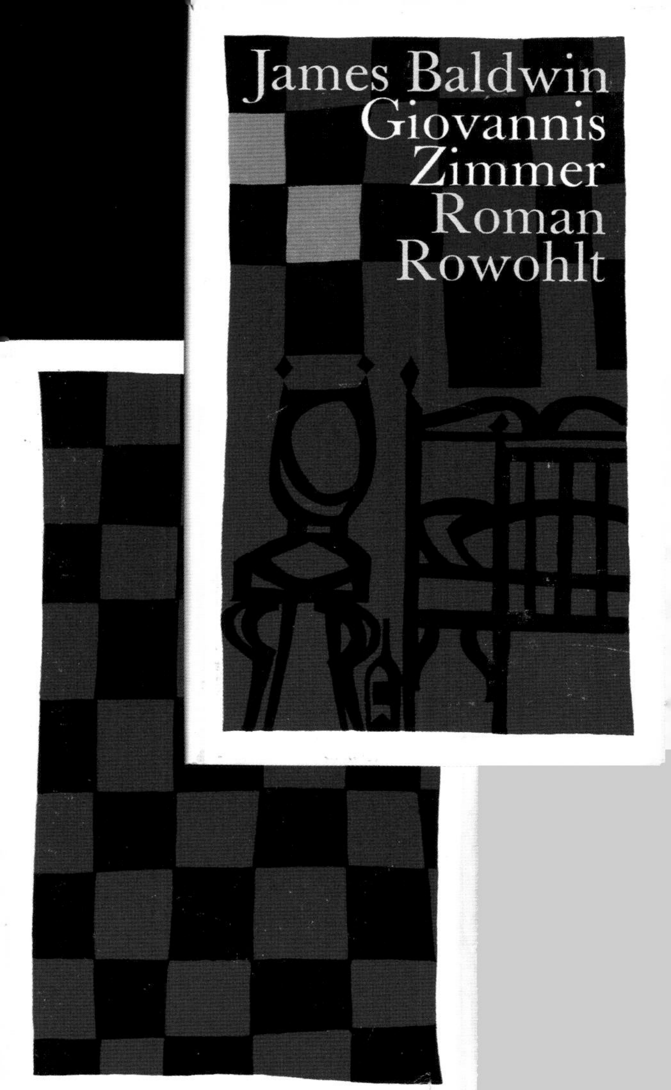
James Baldwin
Giovannis
Zimmer
Roman
Rowohlt

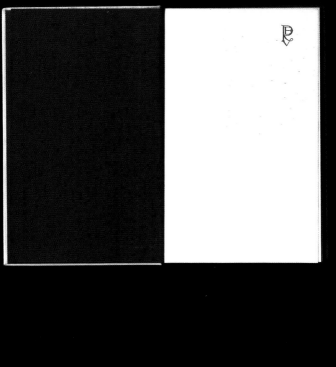

2

Ich weiss nicht recht, wie ich Giovannis Zimmer beschreiben soll. Es wurde irgendwie zu jedem Raum, den ich jemals betreten hatte, und jeder Raum, den ich von nun an betrete, wird mich an jenes Zimmer erinnern. Ich habe dort nicht sehr lange gewohnt – wir lernten uns kennen, bevor der Frühling begann, und schon im Sommer verließ ich Giovanni –, und doch ist mir, als wären es Jahre und Jahrzehnte gewesen. Das Leben in jenem Zimmer schien sich, wie gesagt, unter Wasser abzuspielen, und es steht fest, daß sich auf dem Meeresgrund eine entscheidende Veränderung in mir vollzog.

Das Zimmer war nicht groß genug für zwei. Es gewährte Ausblick auf einen kleinen Hof, was übrigens nichts anderes heißen soll, als daß es zwei Fenster hatte, gegen die sich der Hof, andrängend wie ein Dschungel, Tag für Tag feindselig preßte. Geöffnet wurden die Fenster von uns – oder vielmehr von Giovanni – sehr selten; er hatte nie Gardinen gekauft, und wir kauften auch keine, solange ich bei ihm wohnte. Um vor neugierigen Blicken geschützt zu sein, hatte Giovanni die Scheiben mit einer weißen Reinigungspaste bestrichen. Manchmal hörten wir Kinder auf dem Hof spielen, manchmal zeichneten sich seltsame Schatten vor dem Fenster ab. In solchen Augenblicken pflegte Giovanni, ob er nun im Zimmer arbeitete oder auf dem Bett lag, gleichsam zu erstarren wie ein witternder Hund und re-

gungslos zu warten, bis das, was unsere Sicherheit bedrohte, verschwunden war.

Er steckte immer voller Pläne für die Umgestaltung des Zimmers und hatte auch schon damit angefangen, bevor ich kam. Die eine Wand, von der er die Tapete heruntergerissen hatte, war schmutzigweiß mit helleren und dunkleren Streifen. Die gegenüberliegende Wand wurde nie in Angriff genommen; auf ihr promenierten unentwegt, von Rosen umgeben, eine Dame in einem Reifrock und ein Kavalier in Kniehosen. Die abgerissene Tapete lag in Fetzen und Rollen auf den staubigen Dielen. Auch unsere schmutzige Wäsche, Giovannis Werkzeuge, die Pinsel, die Öl- und Terpentinflaschen waren über den Fußboden verstreut. Unsere Koffer standen übereinandergestapelt, so daß wir uns immer fürchteten, sie zu öffnen. Manchmal vergingen Tage, bevor wir uns dazu aufrafften, Kleinigkeiten, wie etwa saubere Socken, herauszuholen. Niemand besuchte uns, abgesehen von Jacques, und der kam nicht oft. Wir wohnten weit draußen und hatten kein Telefon.

Ich erinnere mich an den ersten Nachmittag, an dem ich dort erwachte. Giovanni lag neben mir, fest schlafend und schwer wie ein Felsen. Das Sonnenlicht drang so schwach in den Raum, daß ich nicht wußte, wie spät es war. Vorsichtig, denn ich wollte Giovanni nicht wecken, zündete ich mir eine Zigarette an. Ich wußte noch nicht, wie ich seinem Blick begegnen sollte. Ich schaute mich um. Giovanni hatte im Taxi erwähnt, daß sein Zimmer sehr schmutzig sei. «Davon bin ich überzeugt», hatte ich leichthin erwidert und mich abgewandt, um aus dem Fenster zu sehen. Dann hatten wir beide geschwiegen. Als ich in seinem Zimmer aufwachte, erinnerte ich mich an dieses Schweigen, in dem etwas Gespanntes und Schmerzliches gelegen hatte und das erst gebrochen wurde, als Giovanni mit einem scheuen, bitteren Lächeln sagte: «Ich muß ein dichterisches Bild finden.»

Seine Finger griffen in die Luft und schienen dort eine Metapher erhaschen zu wollen. Ich beobachtete ihn, bis er schließlich weitersprach.

"Nearly all strata of American black society have found their prophet in Fanon."*

"Fanon was and is an effective, articulate voice of the oppressed, of the black man who suffers the dominance of white 'superiority,' of the native locked in mortal contest with the settler, the oppressor. Fanon's voice is black and intellectual, but it is one with which all the brothers can identify, in Nigeria, in Harlem, in Jamaica, in Angola . . ."—*Saturday Review**

". . . The writing of Malcolm or Cleaver or Amiri Baraka (LeRoi Jones) or the Black Panther leaders, reveals how profoundly they have been moved by the thoughts of a man who went to Paris intending to become a dentist rather than a radical firebrand. . . . Peter Geismar's biography is notably cool and has well-marshalled qualities necessary in handling the issues of our abrasive, dislocated times. . . *Fanon* is an illuminating study . . ."—*The Boston Globe*

"The first full scale biography of the author of *The Wretched of the Earth*. . . . Geismar draws an intriguing portrait of Fanon as an angry, dedicated young intellectual . . ."

—*Publishers' Weekly*

". . . adept and perceptive. . . . After reading it one fully knows Fanon . . ."—*Playboy*

PRINTED IN U.S.A.

394-17396-1

B-350 $1.95

FANON

the Revolutionary as Prophet

a biography by Peter Geismar

FANON

I. Books (American Editions)

F. Fanon, *A Dying Colonialism*. New York: Grove Press, 1968.
———, *Black Skin, White Masks*. New York: Grove Press, 1967.
———, *Toward the African Revolution*. New York: Grove Press, 1969. (Includes most of Fanon's articles in *El Moudjahid*, 1957–1962).
———, *The Wretched of the Earth*. New York: Grove Press, 1968.

II. Medical Articles

F. Fanon, "Réflexions sur la ethnopsychiatrie." *Conscience Maghrebine*, No. 3, (1955).
———, "Le Phénomène de l'agitation en milieu psychiatrique. Considérations générales—signification psychopathologique," *Maroc Medical* (January, 1957).
——— and C. Geronomi, "L'Hôpitalisation de jour en psychiatrie. Valeur et limites." *La Tunisie Médicale*, No. 10 (1959).
——— and ———, "Le T.A.T. chez la femme musulmane. Sociologie de la perception et de l'imagination." Congrès de médecins aliénistes et neurologues de France et des pays de langue française (Bordeaux, August 30-September 4, 1956).
——— and F. Sanchez, "Attitude de musulman maghrebin devant la folie." *Revue pratique de psychologie de la vie sociale et d'hygiene mentale*, No. 1 (1956).
——— and F. Tosquelles, "Sur quelques cas traités par la méthode de Bini." Congrès des médecins aliénistes et neurologues de France et des pays de langue française (Pau, July 20–26, 1953).

——— and ———, "Sur un essai de réadaptation chez une malade avec epilepsie morphéique et troubles de caractère grave." Congrès des médecins aliénistes et neurologues de France et des pays de langue française, (Pau, July 20–26, 1953).
——— and ———, "Indications de thérapeutique de Bini dans le cadre des therapeutiques institutionelles." Congrès des médecins aliénistes et neurologues de France et des pays de langue française (Pau, July 20–26, 1953).
——— and J. Azoulay, "La Socialthérapie dans un service d'hommes musulmans," *L'Information Psychiatrique*, No. 9 (1954).
———, J. Dequeker, R. Lacaton, M. Nucci, and F. Ramée, "Aspects actuels de l'assistance mentale en Algérie." *L'Information Psychiatrique* No. 1 (1955).
——— and L. Lèvy, "Premiers essais de Méprobamate injectable dans les états hypocondriaques." *La Tunisie Médicale*, No. 3 (1959).
——— and ———, "A propos d'un cas de spasm de torsion." *La Tunisie Médicale*, No. 9 (1958).
——— and M. Despinoy, "A propos de syndrome de Cotard avec balancement psychosomatique." *Les Annales Médico-Psychologiques*, No. 2 (June, 1953).
———, M. Despinoy, and W. Zenner, "Note sur les techniques de cures de sommeil avec conditionnement et controle electro-encéphalographique." Congrès des médecins aliénistes et neurologues de France et des pays de langue française (Pau, July 20–26, 1953).
——— and R. Lacaton, "Conduites d'aveu en Afrique du

FANON

Peter
Geismar

GROVE PRESS, INC.,
NEW YORK

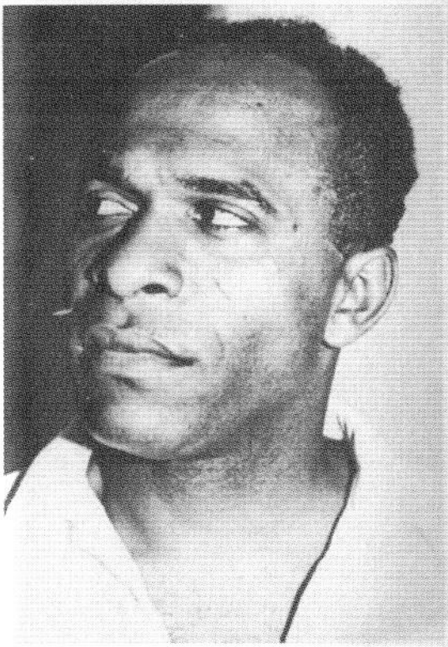

Courtesy Algerian Ministry of Information.

Frantz Fanon in 1959.

ISBN 978-3-9817475-6-0
24 EURO

TRADEMARK
PUBLISHING

Copy, right?

An homage to the Backenzahn™ by ________ Antonia Henschel with a text by ________ Markus Frenzl. Photocopies based on original photographs by ________ Ingmar Kurth.

TRADEMARK
PUBLISHING

Copy, right?

An homage to the Backenzahn™ by
________ Antonia Henschel
with a text by
________ Markus Frenzl.
Photocopies based on original photographs by
________ Ingmar Kurth.

TRADEMARK
PUBLISHING

On genuine and fake back teeth

English Text: Markus Frenzl

Four blocks of wood, each angled on two sides, connected to one another such that the angled sides run together on the inside, the overall body thus tapers downward and a thin cross-shaped seam arises on the seat itself. Simple geometry. And an archaic presence. Surely, that's easy for the cats to copy! As soon as the molar stool hit the markets, there were those imitating it. For 20 years now there have repeatedly been copies and quotes of the seemingly simple design. In cheap furniture stores and even in the more up-market solid-wood furniture makers, copied by local carpenters or made of exotic wood somewhere in the Far East, as the high-end version with no knots, without the trace of a seam or with far too great a distance between the individual elements, with shortened stumpy legs, with exposed tooth necks, with distorted proportions. Countless copies of the Backenzahn™ stool pay illegal reverence to a true classic. Some of them are almost touching in their clumsy awkwardness. Some are eager-to-please copies. Some brashly claim to be originals. The molar-shaped and named stool that Philipp Mainzer designed back in 1996 became a statement almost overnight, one that very many wanted to make their own. Even if they had not come up with it first.

It arose from a wish to make good use of leftovers: When cutting the square heartwood legs for a Bigfoot™ table, there were always bits left that were simply too beautiful to throw away. Clamped together, four of them formed a stool, and its poignant symbolic character soon developed a life of its own, something that could be interpreted as expressing any number of different design trends: As proof of the rediscovery of oak and solid wood. As a sign of the renewed link between contemporary design and craftsmanship. As testimony to the yearning for a more natural, authentic life in the age of digitalization. As an object that stood as much for a reduction to the essentials as it did for the wish for longevity that arose in the wake of the short-lived trends of the 1980s. It thus only logically took its place among the ranks of the straightforward stools in design history and was soon included in design collections in several museums. And like the Ulm Stool designed in 1954 by Max Bill, Hans Gugelot and Paul Hildinger, it stands out for its formal simplicity and

Languages and scripts (written languages) play an important role in forging national identities and turning them into nation states (or vice versa). These imagined communities of people who think, speak, read, and write the same language form closed groups which often stand against one another.

National Letters zooms out from the relatively homogeneous and well-known Western world, and explores four states who use what we could call a *national script* – Isræl, Georgia, Turkey, and Ethiopia – via four case studies.

Using images, texts, and archival material, we can comprehensively explore the past, present, and future of these different typographic landscapes, and come closer to understanding how languages and scripts influence our lives.

With texts and contributions by
Rusudan Amirejibi-Mullen
Ivo T. Budil
Birol Caymaz
Tomáš Garrigue Masaryk
Marek Nedelka
William Safran
Emmanuel Szurek

Edited & Designed by Marek Nedelka
Published by Letter Books

ISBN 978-80-270-9849-1

NATIONAL LETTERS

mutations of H&M, McDonald's, Under Armour, Puma, Makita, etc. [fig.56]. The intimately familiar epigraphic of these global brands, through a simple substitution of the shapes we know so well, feels like a surreal alternate reality somewhere in the Caucasus Mountains. What you'll barely see, however, are signs in Cyrillic script. Although Georgia was indelibly a part of the Soviet Union, the Union could never suppress the historic relationship of the Georgians to their writing system – especially not here, at the very heart of the Georgian nation. Animosity towards Russia was only heightened during the war for South Ossetia in 2008, and type is thus a symbolic (intentional and organic) demonstration of control over one's own territory, and the viability of Georgia's national type and its typographic landscape.

[fig.56] Two examples of the shop signs of international companies using the national *Mkhedruli* script in the streets of Tbilisi – H&M (left) and *Dunkin' Donuts* (right).

Let us now explore for the third time the beginnings of a national movement and the importance of language and writing, this time from the perspective of Georgian linguist Rusudan Amirejibi-Mullen.

Language and Identity in Georgia Under Russian Rule

Rusudan Amirejibi-Mullen

Language has been recognized as a powerful marker of Georgian national identity - *kartveloba* (Georgianness). Georgia is a multi-ethnic and multilingual country and the process of its transformation into a political nation after the collapse of the USSR has been not easy and is still not complete. The reason for this lies, on the one hand, in the Soviet legacy of institutionalised ethnonationalism and, on the other hand, in a strong sense of *kartveloba*, deeply rooted in the pre-Soviet past.

While nationalism is a modern phenomenon, taking historical approach, focusing on political, cultural and linguistic dimensions of nation formation over the longue durée help to elaborate inclusive language and ethnic policies in contemporary Georgia. This study examines Georgia under Russian rule which made the country vulnerable to ethnic conflicts.

The nineteenth century, the epoch of the emergence of modern nations and nationalisms in Europe, also signalled a new stage in the development of *kartveloba* (Georgianness). Notably, the first steps towards becoming a modern nation were made. This social

[fig. 83] The National Council of Georgia declaring Georgia's independence in the main hall of the Vice-regent Palace. Source: National Archives of Georgia.

Drœba and *Iveria* regularly alerted their readers to events in Europe and national-liberation movements in various parts of the world, although the *tergdaleulni*'s movement sought the regeneration of the historic and linguistic community rather than independence. Nevertheless, it is impossible to overestimate the *tergdaleulni*'s role in shaping modern Georgian identity. As Jones (2005: 31) states, they were a vital link to Georgia's Social Democrats, who combined the *tergdaleulni*'s ideas with socialist ideas.

In this respect Georgian Social Democrats or Mensheviks, who were also nationalist (Jones 2005: 2), shared the concerns of the *tergdaleulni*, considering cultural autonomy the best way to secure national self-determination. Before the October Revolution (1917) no single party in Georgia supported political autonomy. Nevertheless, shortly after the Revolution, the head of the Social Democrats, Nœ Zhordania, led the country to independence (Jones 2005: 234–266).

Independent Georgia

The *tergdaleulni* movement was challenged by a younger educated generation of the Marxists in the beginning of the twentieth century. The formation of different political parties in Georgia was a natural consequence of capitalism, which progressed slowly. After almost a century of Russian rule, roads remained unpaved and impassable in winter. The first hospital was built only in 1872 (Jones 2005: 12). The building of factories was restricted, since Russia viewed Georgia as a mere supplier of raw resources and a market for Russian goods. By the beginning of the twentieth century, there were only about thirty factories in Georgia (Gachechiladze 1995: 28). Nevertheless, the political culture of the population was growing and several political parties emerged. Among them, the Social Democrats were the largest and most popular among Georgians. Drawing on Caucasian traditions of cœxistence and cooperation, the Georgian Social Democrats were able to develop an appealing ideology

[fig. 84] One of the first stamps of the Democratic Republic of Georgia, 26 May 1919. Inscribed in French, the official language of the Universal Postal Union, and Georgian Mkhedruli script. Source: Wikimedia Commons.

Hand aufs Herz, Sie kennen den BARON MUNCHHAUSEN nicht? Dessen Schicksal es ist, daß die wildesten und gefährlichsten Bestien ihn gerade angreifen, wenn er außerstande ist, ihnen die Spitze zu bieten? Er aber fährt wohlgemut auf Wölfe, Füchse, entsetzliche Bären mit offenen Rachen, Löwen, Krokodile zu, mit einer Kette Enten durch die Luft, außerdem auf einer Kanonenkugel hin und her oder an einigen fliegenden Männern und Weibern vorbei, die in der Luft Menuett tanzen oder Springerkünste machen und dergleichen Kleinigkeiten, oder auf einem billardkugelförmigen Luftgefährt unendlich hoch am Mond vorbei, wenn er nicht an einer Bohnenranke auf ihn klettert oder im Mittelländischen Meer von einem Fisch verschluckt wird oder den zwei lebenden Hälften seines Pferdes hinterher ist oder in einen Hafen segelt, der mit vortrefflich schmeckender Milch angefüllt ist, oder um eine Insel, die aus einem Käse besteht, oder... Hand aufs Herz, Sie kennen den Baron Münchhausen nicht? – aber tatsächlich nicht gewußt haben Sie möglicherweise, daß es GOTTFRIED AUGUST BURGER (1747–1794) war, dem wir die Geschichten in dieser Fassung verdanken, als ein Volksbuch, dessen Held sprichwörtlich wurde.

BELLETRISTIK

MIT ILLUSTRATIONEN

DDR 1,50 M

UNIVERSAL
Gottfried
August Bürger
MÜNCH-
HAUSEN
ERZÄHLT
Reclam
BIBLIOTHEK

Gottfried August Bürger

WUNDERBARE REISEN ZU WASSER UND LANDE, FELDZÜGE UND LUSTIGE ABENTEUER DES FREIHERRN VON MÜNCHHAUSEN

Wie er dieselben bei der Flasche im Zirkel seiner Freunde selbst zu erzählen pflegt

1983

Verlag Philipp Reclam jun. Leipzig

weniger regierten sie so löblich, daß, wie ich in der Folge erfuhr, niemand Gurken aß, ohne zu sprechen: Gott erhalte den Kaziken.

Nachdem wir unser Schiff, das von diesem Sturme nicht wenig beschädigt war, wieder ausgebessert und uns von dem neuen Monarchen und seiner Gemahlin beurlaubt hatten, segelten wir mit ziemlichem Winde ab und kamen nach sechs Wochen glücklich zu Ceylon an.

Es mochten ungefähr vierzehn Tage seit unserer Ankunft verstrichen sein, als mir der älteste Sohn des Gouverneurs den Vorschlag tat, mit ihm auf die Jagd zu gehen, den ich auch herzlich gern annahm. Mein Freund war ein großer, starker Mann und an die Hitze jenes Klimas gewöhnt; ich aber wurde in kurzer Zeit und bei ganz mäßiger Bewegung so matt, daß ich, als wir in den Wald gekommen waren, weit hinter ihm zurückblieb.

Ich wollte mich eben an dem Ufer eines reißenden Stromes, der schon einige Zeit meine Aufmerksamkeit beschäftigt hatte, niedersetzen, um mich etwas auszuruhen, als ich auf einmal auf dem Wege, den ich gekommen war, ein Geräusch hörte. Ich sah zurück und wurde fast versteinert, als ich einen ungeheueren Löwen erblickte, der gerade auf mich zukam und mich nicht undeutlich merken ließ, daß er gnädigst geruhe, meinen armen Leichnam zu seinem Frühstücke zu machen, ohne sich nur meine Einwilligung auszubitten. Meine Flinte war bloß mit Hasenschrot geladen. Langes Besinnen erlaubte mir weder die Zeit noch meine Verwirrung. Doch entschloß ich mich, auf die Bestie zu feuern, in der Hoffnung, sie zu schrecken, vielleicht auch zu verwunden. Allein da ich in der Angst nicht einmal wartete, bis mir der Löwe zum Schusse kam, so wurde er dadurch wütend gemacht und kam nun mit aller Heftigkeit auf mich los. Mehr aus Instinkt als aus vernünftiger Überlegung versuchte ich eine Unmöglichkeit — zu entfliehen. Ich kehre mich um, und — mir läuft noch, sooft ich daran gedenke, ein kalter Schauder über den Leib — wenige Schritte vor mir steht ein scheußlicher Krokodil, der schon fürchterlich seinen Rachen aufsperrte, um mich zu verschlingen.

Stellen Sie sich, meine Herren, das Schreckliche meiner Lage vor! Hinter mir der Löwe, vor mir der Krokodil, zu meiner Linken ein reißender Strom, zu meiner Rechten ein Abgrund, in dem, wie ich nachher hörte, die giftigsten Schlangen sich aufhielten.

Betäubt — und das war einem Herkules in dieser Lage nicht übelzunehmen — stürze ich zu Boden. Jeder Gedanke, den meine Seele noch vermochte, war die schreckliche Erwartung, jetzt die Zähne oder Klauen des wütenden Raubtiers zu fühlen oder in dem Rachen des Krokodils zu stekken. Doch in wenigen Sekunden hörte ich einen starken, aber durchaus fremden Laut. Ich wage es endlich, meinen Kopf aufzuheben und mich umzuschauen, und — was meinen Sie? — zu meiner unaussprechlichen Freude finde ich, daß der Löwe in der Hitze, in der er auf mich losschoß, in eben dem Augenblicke, in dem ich niederstürzte, über mich weg in den Rachen des Krokodils gesprungen war. Der Kopf des einen steckte nun in dem Schlunde des andern, und sie strebten mit aller Macht, sich voneinander loszumachen. Gerade noch zu rechter Zeit sprang ich auf, zog meinen Hirschfänger, und mit einem Streiche haute ich den Kopf des Löwen ab, so daß der Rumpf zu meinen Füßen zuckte. Darauf rammte ich mit dem untern Ende meiner Flinte den Kopf noch tiefer in den Rachen des Krokodils, der nun jämmerlich ersticken mußte.

Bald nachdem ich diesen vollkommenen Sieg über zwei fürchterliche Feinde erfochten hatte, kam mein Freund, um zu sehen, was die Ursache meines Zurückbleibens wäre.

Nach gegenseitigen Glückwünschen maßen wir den Krokodil und fanden ihn genau vierzig Pariser Fuß sieben Zoll lang.

Sobald wir dem Gouverneur dieses außerordentliche Abenteuer erzählet hatten, schickte er einen Wagen mit einigen Leuten aus und ließ die beiden Tiere nach seinem Hause holen. Aus dem Felle des Löwen mußte mir ein dortiger Kürschner Tobaksbeutel verfertigen, von denen ich einige meinen Bekannten zu Ceylon verehrte. Mit den übrigen machte ich bei unserer Rückkunft nach Holland Geschenke an die Bürgermeister, die mir dagegen ein Geschenk von tausend Dukaten machen wollten, das ich nur mit vieler Mühe ablehnen konnte.

Die Haut des Krokodils wurde auf die gewöhnliche Art ausgestopft und macht nun eine der größten Merkwürdigkeiten in dem Museum zu Amsterdam aus, wo der Vorzeiger die ganze Geschichte jedem, den er herumführet, erzählt. Dabei macht er denn freilich immer einige Zusätze, von denen verschiedene Wahrheit und Wahrscheinlichkeit in hohem Grade beleidigen. So pflegt er zum Exempel zu sagen, daß der Löwe durch den

Writers in Zimbabwe talk less to each other about their craft than perhaps they should. *Some Writers Can Give You Two Heartbeats* is an eclectic and indispensable treasury of wisdom from Zimbabwe's literary masters cleverly brought together to dialogue with each other about issues that speak to their common history and vocation. It's an inventive and groundbreaking book that reimagines the art of conversation erased of the clichés, plot summaries and rote commentary that form the bulk of slapdash author Q&As we see so frequently. This book is a gathering of minds discussing their writing and methods with candidness found nowhere else. They do not always agree, or look at things the same way. Literature, we are reminded, is disputed territory.

Tinashe Mushakavanhu

ISBN 978-0-7974-9573-9

9 780797 495739 >

258

Some Writers Can Give You Two Heartbeats

Edited by Tinashe Mushakavanhu
with Nontsikelelo Mutiti

Dambudzo Marechera: *An Imaginary Conversation*

It is reported that in 1978, Dambudzo Marechera, heckled Robert Mugabe when he came to London to address Zimbabweans at the Africa Centre. He had already seen the troubles ahead. Marechera could read through the deceptive characters that were on the brink of leading Zimbabwe. Most of them were his contemporaries and former classmates. His award-winning book, The House of Hunger, had just been published. In this imaginary conversation, Tinashe Mushakavanhu, finds out what kind of things Marechera would be saying about his country and its endless crises. What would Dambudzo Marechera be saying is a speculative question that elicits many responses? But here are some of Marechera's insights extracted from his own books and published interviews.

Tinashe Mushakavanhu:

Where does the problem lie in Zimbabwe? Who is to blame for the crisis in Zimbabwe today?

Dambudzo Marechera:

We in Zimbabwe know who the enemy is. The enemy is just not white, he is also black. The police force, the army in Zimbabwe are three-quarters black. They have always been. And for me I believe that to see the Zimbabwe struggle as merely a black versus white struggle is stupid and naive. And hence, in most of my work, there's always a mistrust of politicians, no matter who they are.

TM: Zimbabwe has been constantly in the news as a kind of hell on earth. What is the actual state of affairs in Zimbabwe?

Above:
After Dambudzo Marechera's sister, Tsitsi, was killed with a parcel bomb in Harare, Robert Mugabe led a government delegation to pay their condolences to the writer.

DAMBUDZO MARECHERA

I usually – in a childish way – protest, when they arrest me saying 'Look I'm just a writer. I'm not carrying guns against you. Why don't you just leave me alone to write my books in any way I want?' A pen is not a gun. A gun will actually kill somebody but a pen can stimulate thought and in this sense the pen should be given unlimited freedom.

IRENE STAUNTON

I think one can safely say that there is no censorship of fiction in Zimbabwe, possibly because so very few people buy books that the state has little to fear from them. Certainly censorship does not seem to affect how people write, whether they are published or unpublished. A good writer has a sense of integrity that is hard to compromise. That being said, fear is a palpable force. One may try to counter it with Churchillian sternness by telling oneself that 'there is nothing to fear but fear itself'; I suspect this provides little real comfort: fear is unfortunately a contagious force.

KIZITO MUCHEMWA

Any writer worth her salt has to find strategies of survival. Every regime has it's own sophisticated ways of censorship and writers have to find strategies of beating these strategies. Good writing will emerge no matter how repressive a regime can be. Good writing will survive. Writing that does not seek to beat these strategies of censorship will end up, as an appendage to the department of propaganda.

Allen Ginsberg's *HOWL AND OTHER POEMS* was originally published by City Lights Books in the Fall of 1956. Subsequently seized by U.S. customs and the San Francisco police, it was the subject of a long court trial at which a series of poets and professors persuaded the court that the book was not obscene.

Allen Ginsberg was born June 3, 1926, the son of Naomi Ginsberg, Russian émigré, and Louis Ginsberg, lyric poet and schoolteacher, in Paterson, N.J. To these facts Ginsberg adds: "High school in Paterson till 17, Columbia College, merchant marine, Texas and Denver, copyboy, Times Square, amigos in jail, dishwashing, book reviews, Mexico City, market research, Satori in Harlem, Yucatan and Chiapas 1954, West Coast 3 years. Later Arctic Sea trip, Tangier, Venice, Amsterdam, Paris, read at Oxford Harvard Columbia Chicago, quit, wrote *Kaddish* 1959, made tape to leave behind & fade in Orient awhile. Carl Solomon to whom *HOWL* is addressed, is an intuitive Bronx dadaist and prose-poet."

Later books by Allen Ginsberg in the Pocket Poets Series: *KADDISH And Other Poems, REALITY SANDWICHES, PLANET NEWS, THE FALL OF AMERICA, MIND BREATHS*, and *PLUTONIAN ODE*.

$7.95
ISBN 978-0-87286-017-9
50795>
9 780872 860179

$7.95

CITY LIGHTS

THE POCKET POETS SERIES

HOWL

AND OTHER POEMS

ALLEN GINSBERG

Introduction by

William Carlos Williams

NUMBER FOUR

HOWL
AND OTHER POEMS
BY
ALLEN GINSBERG
'Unscrew the locks from the doors!
Unscrew the doors themselves from their jambs!'
CITY LIGHTS BOOKS
San Francisco

who cowered in unshaven rooms in underwear, burning their money in wastebaskets and listening to the Terror through the wall,
who got busted in their pubic beards returning through Laredo with a belt of marijuana for New York,
who ate fire in paint hotels or drank turpentine in Paradise Alley, death, or purgatoried their torsos night after night
with dreams, with drugs, with waking nightmares, alcohol and cock and endless balls,
incomparable blind streets of shuddering cloud and lightning in the mind leaping toward poles of Canada & Paterson, illuminating all the motionless world of Time between,
Peyote solidities of halls, backyard green tree cemetery dawns, wine drunkenness over the rooftops, storefront boroughs of teahead joyride neon blinking traffic light, sun and moon and tree vibrations in the roaring winter dusks of Brooklyn, ashcan rantings and kind king light of mind,
who chained themselves to subways for the endless ride from Battery to holy Bronx on benzedrine until the noise of wheels and children brought them down shuddering mouth-wracked and battered bleak of brain all drained of brilliance in the drear light of Zoo,

who sank all night in submarine light of Bickford's floated out and sat through the stale beer afternoon in desolate Fugazzi's, listening to the crack of doom on the hydrogen jukebox,
who talked continuously seventy hours from park to pad to bar to Bellevue to museum to the Brooklyn Bridge,
a lost battalion of platonic conversationalists jumping down the stoops off fire escapes off windowsills off Empire State out of the moon,
yacketayakking screaming vomiting whispering facts and memories and anecdotes and eyeball kicks and shocks of hospitals and jails and wars,
whole intellects disgorged in total recall for seven days and nights with brilliant eyes, meat for the Synagogue cast on the pavement,
who vanished into nowhere Zen New Jersey leaving a trail of ambiguous picture postcards of Atlantic City Hall,
suffering Eastern sweats and Tangerian bone-grindings and migraines of China under junk-withdrawal in Newark's bleak furnished room,
who wandered around and around at midnight in the railroad yard wondering where to go, and went, leaving no broken hearts,

WILD ORPHAN

Blandly mother
takes him strolling
by railroad and by river
—he's the son of the absconded
hot rod angel—
and he imagines cars
and rides them in his dreams,

so lonely growing up among
the imaginary automobiles
and dead souls of Tarrytown

to create
out of his own imagination
the beauty of his wild
forebears—a mythology
he cannot inherit.

Will he later hallucinate
his gods? Waking
among mysteries with
an insane gleam
of recollection?

The recognition—
something so rare
in his soul,
met only in dreams
—nostalgias
of another life.

A question of the soul.
And the injured
losing their injury
in their innocence
—a cock, a cross,
an excellence of love.

And the father grieves
in flophouse
complexities of memory
a thousand miles
away, unknowing
of the unexpected
youthful stranger
bumming toward his door.

New York, April 13, 1952

With contributions by Nana Adusei-Poku, Ricardo Basbaum, Frédérique Bergholtz, Eric C.H. de Bruyn, Binna Choi, David Dibosa, Denise Ferreira da Silva, Avery F. Gordon, Tom Holert, Nataša Ilić, Charl Landvreugd, Sven Lütticken, Anna Manubens, Ruth Noack, Emily Pethick, Grant Watson

IRRUPTION

Dr. A.H. Heineken prijs voor de Kunst 2014

Amateur

Wendelien van Oldenborgh

proposition-program.... THAT WHICH IS PROPOSED IS ALWAYS GIVEN AS PLAY...CHANCE-PLAY...BY THE THROW OF A DICE AND NEVER AS A FIXATION ON EXISTING MODELS: PARTICIPATION AS INVENTION: SCRAMBLING OF THE ROLES: JOYFUL...... WITHOUT SWEAT.

AMATEUR
WENDELIEN VAN OLDENBORGH
Sternberg Press
The Showroom
If I Can't Dance, I Don't Want To Be Part Of Your Revolution

Prologue: In Front of the Capturing Device

In 1985, Jean Genet was interviewed by Nigel Williams for the BBC. The interview was filmed in London over two days. On the second day, Genet tells his interviewer that he has had a dream:

> I dreamed that the technicians for this film revolted. Assisting with the arrangement of the shots, the preparation of a film, they never have the right to speak. And I thought they would be daring enough – since we were talking yesterday about being daring – to chase me from my seat, to take my place. And yet they don't move.[1]

Genet asks Williams to check with his crew. We briefly get a glimpse of the technicians. Their stiff perplexity is relieved by Williams's redirection of the situation in a psychoanalytical manner: 'Is this what interests you about your dream: disrupting the order of things?' To which Genet replies:

> Obviously I want to disrupt the order. I told you yesterday that you were doing the work of a cop and you've already forgotten it, because you continue to interrogate me just like the thief I was thirty years ago was interrogated by the police. [...] There is a norm on one side, a norm where you are, all of you... and then there's an outer margin where I am marginalised. And am I afraid of entering the norm? Of course I'm afraid of entering the norm, and if I'm raising my voice right now, it's because I'm in the process of entering the norm.[2]

In assimilating the interview with a police interrogation, Genet is pointing at the power structure that underlies an interview and, more generally, a TV set or a filming situation. A mode of summarising his point would be to say that a camera is a *capturing device*. The formulation refers to both its technical description – as a recorder – and to a

1 Extract from BBC 'Omnibus' interview with Jean Genet broadcasted on 12 November 1985, available at http://www.bbc.co.uk/programmes/p00kvnwv (last accessed on 21 February 2015).

2 *Ibid.*

critical perception of its imprisoning capacity. The double meaning reflects Genet's uneasiness towards the filming apparatus's inherent authority and normativity, characteristics that become especially violent when the filmed subject is withdrawn from the decision over the ways in which he or she will be framed.

In watching the full interview, it becomes apparent that what Genet is explicitly affirming at this point was already implicit in his previous answers and general attitude. In addition to repeatedly stressing the prejudices behind Williams's questions he consistently tries to reverse the interviewer-interviewee dialectic through abrupt interruptions: 'What about you? Do you prefer to keep at a distance?'

This idea of 'distance', as well as that of the normative power underpinning a filming process, provides an interesting way to consider Wendelien van Oldenborgh's recent (film) project,[3] *Beauty and the Right to the Ugly* (2014). Van Oldenborgh chose to position herself *within* the filmed situation as opposed to standing safely *in front of it*, a methodology that was progressively set in motion, and which mirrors the issues that the project intended to explore. In other words, the way in which she worked became a translation of the architectural – and in fact political – premises that were at stake, into a film-making methodology.

Having worked with the artist over the course of a year on the conceptual and practical development of the piece, my viewpoint is informed by a close involvement in the successive phases that led to the film. Observing the process as a form of action that spans beyond the capsule of its result (the film), what follows is an attempt to unpack the singularity of that process by focusing precisely on how distance and filming norms were handled by the artist.

The Ugly and Noise

The Karregat was a radical architectural and social experiment designed in 1972 by the Dutch architect Frank van Klingeren. The building was – or sought to be – a multifunctional community centre in a neighbourhood of new housing designed for

3 The parentheses highlight the fact that what follows is a reflection that encompasses both the film and – maybe even more importantly – the process that led to it.

on *Beauty and the Right to the Ugly*, 2014

STILL Bele & Dewe

STILL Bele & Dewe

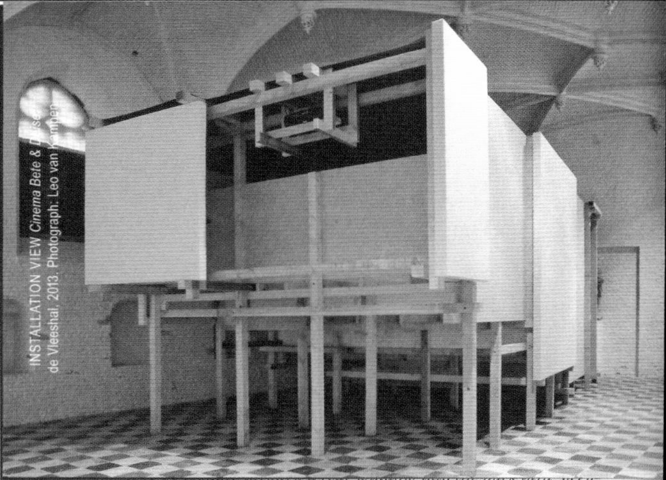

INSTALLATION VIEW *Cinema Bete & Deise*, de Vleeshal, 2013. Photograph: Leo van Kampen

ing on the woman.

The next frame shows three glassless windows from inside a building in daytime; one can glimpse through the window and recognise a backyard. Open window frames, a building under construction; something is about to materialise, to become. Nonetheless, there remains a sense of cessation. The woman's voice whispers rhythmically, aspirates, almost singing: 'I came from Brazil to do a tour in Europe, missing it terrible, cock on my mind afraid of making mistakes in Portuguese, I had forgotten that it is only English I cannot speak.' The perspective shifts; the viewer encounters the same empty window frames from the outside whilst the voice continues to sing and whisper the words.

These are the first scenes from Wendelien van Oldenborgh's 2012 film *Bete & Deise*. The viewer is thrown into the middle of a conversation, which prevents one from determining its location, its starting point, or a clear understanding of the dialogue. I immediately ask myself: Who is here, in dialogue with whom? Is this a dialogue? What is the subject of this dialogue? Who is filming and who is directing; what is the

Who else is there, and who remains outside of the frame?

The opening minutes of the film, which I have just described, reveal that the viewer is thrown into an open structure, a space in transition, a dialogue that includes silent voices, invisible bodies, unspoken comments, avoided subjects and an atemporal narrative. The two women, whose first names give the film its title – Bete Mendes and Deise Tigrona – tell each other parts of their life stories that revolve around very particular events. Something about this confuses me from the beginning: despite their being well disposed to each other, their stories seem at first not to connect, which awakens my curiosity for the subtle tones, the metanarrative of their conversation.

1980s held the elective office of Congresswoman as a member of the Partido dos Trabalhadores (Worke Party). She also held the post of Secretary of Cultur in the state of São Paulo from 1987–88, and became president of the Fundação de Artes do Estado do R de Janeiro (Arts Foundation of the State of Rio de Janeiro) in 1999.

SYNOPSIS *Bete & Deise*

Deise stages an encounter between men in Rio de Janeiro: Bete Mendes ise Tigrona. These women have – their own way – given meaning to a of a public voice. Since the 1960s, s has maintained a political career ide her acting career in popular ion. Mendes was involved in the resistance group of the student nent against the dictatorship, and art of the labour movement in 70s, co-founding the Partido dos nadores, the workers' party that has ise to Brazil's former and current ents, Lula de Silva and Dilma eff. Tigrona, for her part, is one of ost powerful female voices in the Carioca movement. Growing up and ming as a singer in the impoverished unity of Cidade de Deus, she rose at international popularity when her Injeção' was used as the basis .A.'s popular hit 'Bucky Done Gun'. as forced to take a step back when it ne too burdensome to combine her music career with her tough family life in Cidade de Deus. Together these women talk about their experience with performance and their position in the public sphere, allowing for the contradictions that they each carry within themselves to surface.

NEUES LOTES FOLUM®

I/27

ZEITSCHRIFT FÜR DIE POÉSIE UND DIE RÉVOLUTION

ORTSGRUPPE FRANKFURT DAS EDI-
TORIAL – **ORTSGRUPPE BERLIN** DAS
EINTRETEN IN DIE BEGRIFFE – **(PR-ABTEI-
LUNG DER NLF)** EIN PROGRAMM –
AJA ZUTSCHESTOWAWADSCHJU
EINE ERKLARUNG – **A. MIJN JONG**
EIN TAGTRAUM – **G. v. CAMPE** EINE
REVOLTE – **A. SOHN-RETHEL** – EINE
KRITIK – **P. FEYERABEND** EIN DISKURS
– **G. BATAILLE** EIN ENTFALTETER BE-
GRIFF – **REDAKTION** EINE ERFAHRUNG

DM 20,–

Verlag Association GmbH

IMPRESSUM

[illegible]

HERAUSGEBER:
REDAKTIONSKOLLEKTIV-
NEKROPHILIACS LIBERATION FRONT
(ORTSGRUPPEN: AMSTERDAM, BERLIN, [illegible], BREMEN, FRANKFURT, [illegible], LONDON, NEW YORK, [illegible], PARIS, [illegible], WIEN, [illegible])

IM VERLAG:
[illegible]

[illegible]

DORT, WO SICH [illegible] WO MAN SCHREIBT, UM GELIEBT ZU WERDEN, WO MAN LIEBT, UM SCHREIBEN ZU KÖNNEN

INHALT

(EIN MÖGLICHES [illegible])

* * * * *

[illegible]

NEUES LOTES FOLUM®

1/27

ZEITSCHRIFT FÜR DIE POÉSIE UND DIE RÉVOLUTION

ORTSGRUPPE FRANKFURT DAS EDITORIAL – **ORTSGRUPPE BERLIN** DAS EINTRETEN IN DIE BEGRIFFE – **(PR-ABTEILUNG DER NLF)** EIN PROGRAMM – **AJA ZUTSCHESTOWAWADSCHJU** EINE ERKLÄRUNG – **A. MIJN JONG** EIN TAGTRAUM – **G. v. CAMPE** EINE REVOLTE – **A. SOHN-RETHEL** – EINE KRITIK – **P. FEYERABEND** EIN DISKURS – **G. BATAILLE** EIN ENTFALTETER BEGRIFF – **REDAKTION** EINE ERFAHRUNG

Ein Tagtraum
(DARIN EIN PFERD DIE BEGEGNUNG GESTATTETE UND GESTALTETE)

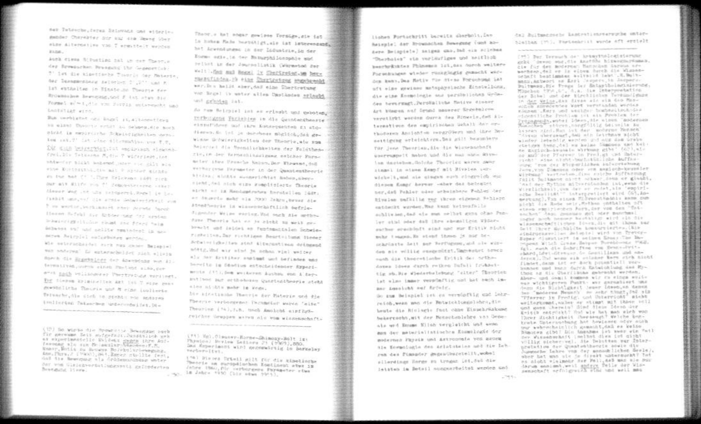

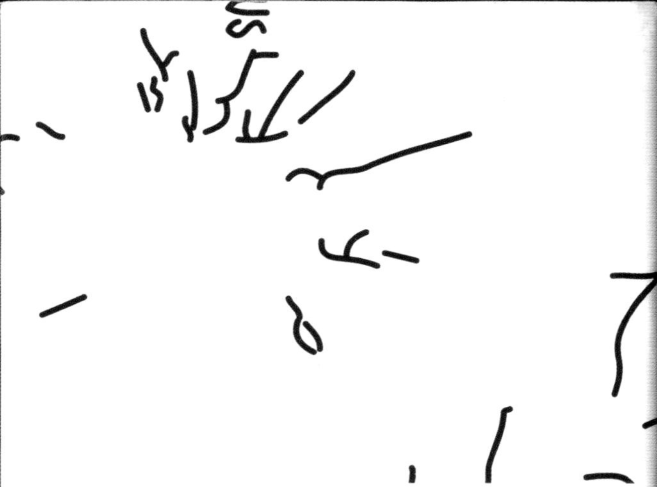

ies Declaiming Kant, 2004)

Journal for Political and Formal
in Art—Issue 4

In the Belly of the Beast—Art and Language
New York Project, 1972–1976

Rab-Rab: Journal for Political and Formal Inquiries in Art

Issue 4.2

Rab–Rab
Issue 4.1

Journal of Political and Formal Inquiries in Art

Fig. 5.

ceremony looks quite different and is called pumping. Inciting is the invitation to permanent pair formation. If the drake is inclined to accept the proposal he lifts his chin, turns his head slightly away from the duck and says very quickly, 'Rabrab, rabrab,' or, especially when he is in the water, he answers with a certain likewise ritualized ceremony: drinking and sham preening. Both these ceremonies mean that the drake mallard is answering, 'I will!' The utterance 'Rabrab' contains an element of aggression, the turning away of the head with lifted chin is a typical gesture of appeasement. If he is very excited, the drake may actually make a small demonstration attack on another drake which chances to be standing near. In the second ceremony,

Remembering as Future

Sezgin Boynik

An Introduction to the Fourth Issue of Rab-Rab Journal

This is an odd and transitional number published in two volumes. Most contributions deal with historical moments that we consider as contemporary. We think that the energy of these moments should be further unleashed and sharpened. At the end of this introduction, we provide a glimpse into a theory regarding the effects of this actualisation.

Despite the whole issue being concerned with the actual reverberations of the past, the opening contribution by Martta Tuomaala, an artist and union activist based in Helsinki, is about today. It starts with a short introduction to her misadventures in exhibiting *Cleaner's Voice*, a multi-screen installation about the position of cleaners in today's Finland, from the perspective of having worked as a cleaner. Tuomaala's text continues with a long rap abstracting the violent capitalist expropriation and primitive accumulation policies implemented by ruling politicians. The consequences are devastating. It results with plundering public wealth and pillaging the much-appreciated nature of Finland.

Minna Henriksson's notes, which are written after presenting two recent artworks, are about "the elite class of intellectuals and 'national artists' who invent and reproduce the ideology of racism by racialising the masses." The outcome is a group portrait of institutions, similar to Dutch group paintings, which expose how compact and rigid the national apparatuses are. Her scratches, in the form of notes and maps, are pointing to a way out by indicating the existence of a different history which does not belong to that of courts and palaces.

These two texts are Rab-Rab's contribution to the ongoing centenary celebrations of the independent bourgeois Finnish state.

Zbyněk Baladrán, the conceptual artist from Prague, replays the old film about the Czechoslovakian velvet revolution, questioning the "logical" justifications of anti-communism and finding nothing but the same old scenario of primitive accumulation. The name of this film, which already tastes sour in Czechia, could have been *A Film of Your Life* as well, firmly guaranteeing the freedom of consumerism under the protectorate of the dictatorship of capital.

Ali Akbar Mehta is interested in colours of violence. In his contribution, we read about how the religious-infected riots in Ayodhya (an ancient city of India) started after the alleged dream of a believer, who channelled the truth received from Rama regarding ownership of the holy place. Mehta witnessed one of these riots as a child in December 1992. They were the first images (the photons) of politics that he processed as an act of collective violence.

In this issue there are four dossiers. The first is about Jacques Rancière, emerging from his summer 2016 visit to Helsinki that we organised together with the collective PhD in One Night. In following the practice of PhD in One Night which follows Rancière's method of equality, we aimed to expand knowledge production to both a horizontal and collective level. The result, which is presented as "eyes, hands, comets, and metagrams", consists of two interviews with Rancière and three interventions. The interview made in Helsinki is about Althusser's lesson, Maoism, class struggles, revolution and experimental art. The second, a forgotten interview with Rancière from the mid-seventies, is taken from *Edinburgh 77 Magazine* an underground film journal published in Edinburgh. This is an abridged version of the original interview which was for the first published in *Cahiers du Cinéma*, questioned the limits of representing history in film, and criticised the revisionist turn from formal experiments towards psychological identifications in seventies cinema. The first intervention is a poetic description of the practice of PhD in One Night, authored by Ivana Momčilović. Spanning Auguste Blanqui's comets to Rosa Luxemburg's herbariums, and from Raymond Roussel's metagrams to 'garlands of words', it is a collage of passionate learning. The analysis of Ranicère's style by Edicija Jugoslavije, a collective publishing platform from Brussels, is yet another insistence on ephemerality pushing the concepts of Rancière towards egalitarianism stemming from communism. Sezgin Boynik's intervention is demounting Karl Hübner's 1844 painting on riots, 'The Silesian Weavers', questions the potentials and limits of what Rancière describes as the unfolding of images, which is understood as the divorce of the eye from the hands. Going back to the foundational texts of communism, the text qualifies the uprising as the philosophical source for young Marx.

The current issue again publishes Alberto Híjar Serrano, Mexican militant theoretician, avant-garde scholar and conceptual artist. Translated by David Muoz (who is editing a full-length book of Serrano's writings for Rab-Rab Press), the essay is a contemporary text on Mexico's centenary of the revolution which questions the superficial applications of "sweeping with the October broom." Muoz also deals with issues of the past by looking at David Alfaro Siqueiros' theories on the formal aspects of political art. He asks about the differences between Walter Benjamin (who never joined the Communist party), and Siqueiros (who was fervent supporter of the official party line). Muoz actualises Siqueiros' complicated conceptualisation of political art's "plástica-monumental-fílmica",

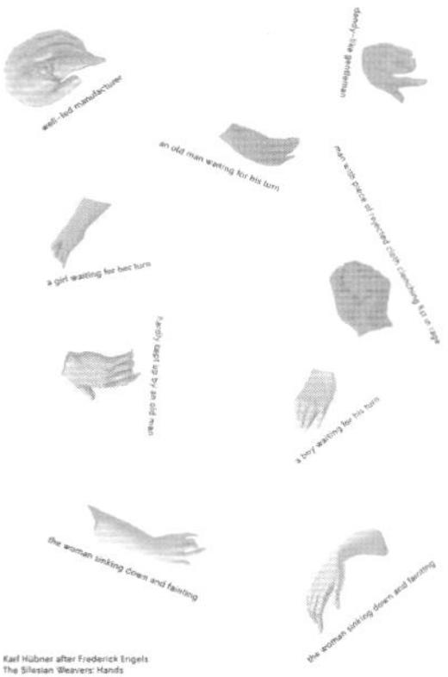

Riot Picture
"Throwing off the political cloak"

Szagün Beyerik

Karl Hübner after Frederick Engels
The Silesian Weavers: Hands

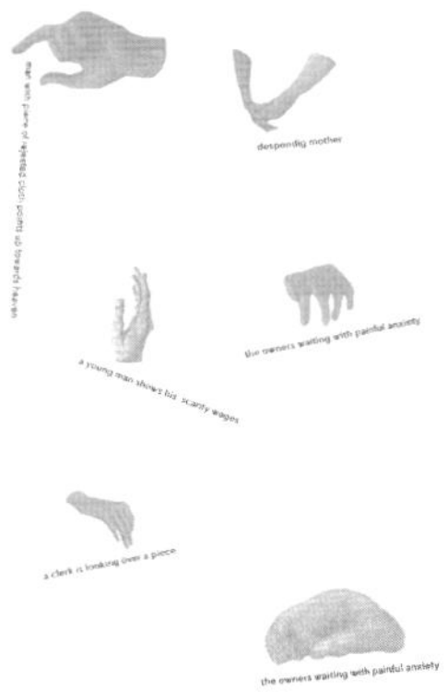

Jacques Rancière
Eyes, Hands, Comets, and Metagrams

access to art by demonstrating a common ground between artist and audience. This common ground had to do with the way experience and the visual interact; we arrange furniture in our living room, and Robert Morris arranges geometric constructions in a gallery. One is just housekeeping or decorating, the other act is art. Long before the institutional theory of art destroyed the epistemological connections that essentialist definitions of art demanded, Dewey argued that the cognitive faculties required for both these acts lie on a continuum, and experience, I think, is the term that denotes an entry point, not the entire process. Everyone has this ability to appreciate the significance of the disposition of forms and colors in space or on a surface. Dewey really didn't separate experience out of the equation, it was central to his epistemology, which we tag simply as pragmatism. Of course, given the power of institutions its not clear that Dewey's "democratic" leveling would necessarily elevate the commonplace as art; it is quite possible that such an analysis of experience would simply strengthen the power of the institution of art to set the terms, and to administer the value of, everyday experience. All that means is that our knowledge is derived from and testable via an empiricist methodology that does not exclude agency. But the confusion that Smith propagated was based on an over-zealous attempt to knock "experience" off its late-Modernist pedestal. The kind of experience of a painting, say, discussed by Greenberg involved an instant of recognition, you got it or you didn't. And when it comes to contemporary art, the term experience generally refers to what I would call "affect". It's all mixed up, and "experience" is far too crude a term.

The linguistic resources in visual art criticism employed to describe experience seem to be quite thin compared with philosophy, psychology, and fiction. At the time, the early-1970s, experience in art was a real buzzword, a trigger word, a polemical fuse we were glad to set alight at any opportunity. So, while I'm quite sure we did not make all the distinctions as fine as we should have, we were not in the business of adhering to any academic criteria. What we wrote, the callow treatment of some concepts you will find in *Blurting in Art & Language*, should be read against the project's polemical purpose, a reflection of our lifeworld that is indexed to the time of its making.

To relate this to the question of the annotations, blurting *as a socializing activity. You are thinking that, let's say, anyone who is not part of your group or collective could join. Was there, let's say, an entry point? What would be entry point to join into your situation?*

I can respond to this in two ways. The first, sounding rather cynical and evasive, though it's not meant to be, is that the notion of "engagement" as first promulgated through Conceptual art differed from what is evident in the work of people like John Cage, Allan Kaprow, or some Fluxus artists. It was not necessarily literal, but a figure of speech, a space opened up for the sake of the participation of the spectator. Another way to respond, which is perhaps what you are more interested in, is to address the question with regard to the expansion, growth, and development of the group thanks to the influx of new people. In that case, the answer is straightforward: one enters the group the same way I did. One makes contact, contributes something, tosses it onto the middle of the table, and becomes part of the social process of meeting, talking, making, and criticizing.

Something like entering through practice, not with a predetermined model, or a set of bureaucratic rules.

That is precisely correct. Art & Language wasn't a club or a fraternity or a cult; my calling it a "gang" was a studied bit of sarcasm that was apparently lost on some. It was about the work, a position, and your willingness to commit yourself to that situation. We did have some turnover, people who drifted in and out. Others who remained associated with the group did very little work indeed. Not everyone was expected to engage in the same activity, we recognized the need for a division of function within our moderately sized community. People did more of what they were good at. At one point in the history of Art & Language it would have been true to say that to work with us you must be able to write essays. But even when we were producing *The Fox*, there was wide latitude concerning what it meant to contribute to the endeavor, from different modes of writing all the way to editorial cartooning.

What about the earlier period, the time of the publication of Blurting in Art & Language New York *(1973)? What can you say about your expectations regarding the response or involvement of readers?*

I think the contents of this publication for an individual outside Art & Language would be whatever they could make of them, just as your response to some of the blurts has some resonance for you at this moment in time. It was conceived along the lines of a handbook to our discourse; to the extent that items in our discourse overlap with your knowledge or interests, then some kind of "conversation" is possible. At least that is one way in which a reader, reflecting on their practice, could make a connection to our practice. The handbook may be like a toolkit to them, whereas for us it has a more vivid, urgent existential life. That is why it has the structure it has, so that we can blur the boundary between "research" and "exposition". It's like an unraveled woolen sweater: now you have the wool, and a guide to the stitches, now make your own style jumper.

You are using the term concatenation frequently. Did you consider this term in relation to the concept of narrative? Because in the beginning of the 1970s, let's say Fredric Jameson and some other Marxist theoreticians, were very much critical of narrative as a dominant form. Was this approach to narrative on your agenda? I raise this question because it seems to me that concatenation is a way to make a picture of a context, a kind of inventory.

I don't think you can link the term concatenation as it was used in Art & Language to the concept of narrative; I prefer to think of it in terms of collage as a means to construct a picture of a context. My interest in historical discourse in art came later, around the time of the publication of the first issue of *The Fox*. I suppose that there was some discussion, even during that period, of something called the "retro-looney-bin", which referred to the problem of reconstructing a "history" of Art & Language and presenting it in a form amenable to the curatorial protocols of the museum retrospective. I wouldn't want to characterize *Blurting in Art & Language* as the narrative of our conversations that took place between January 1973 and June 1973, but that is not to say that we

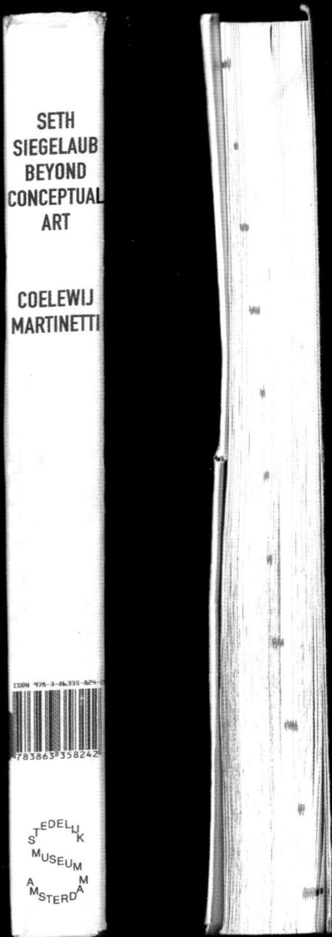
SETH
SIEGELAUB
BEYOND
CONCEPTUAL
ART
COELEWIJ
MARTINETTI
ISBN 978-3-86335-824-2
783863 358242
STEDELIJK
MUSEUM
AMSTERDAM

SETH SIEGELAUB
BEYOND CONCEPTUAL ART

XEROX BOOK
JANUARY 5–31, 1969
ART WITHOUT SPACE
THE HALIFAX CONFERENCE
INTERNATIONAL GENERAL
JULY/AUGUST EXHIBITION
THE ARTIST'S CONTRACT
PUBLIC PRESS + NEWS NETWORK
IMMRC
MARXISM AND THE MASS MEDIA
HOW TO READ DONALD DUCK
COMMUNICATION AND CLASS STRUGGLE
CSROT
BIBLIOGRAPHICA TEXTILIA HISTORIÆ
THE CONTEXT OF ART/THE ART OF CONTEXT
TIME AND CAUSALITY IN PHYSICS
HOW IS ART HISTORY MADE?

STEDELIJK MUSEUM AMSTERDAM

CATALOGUE-AS-EXHIBITION

SETH SIEGELAUB
BEYOND CONCEPTUAL ART

VERLAG DER BUCHHANDLUNG WALTHER KÖNIG, KÖLN
STEDELIJK MUSEUM AMSTERDAM
2016

MY GALLERY IS THE WORLD NOW

EXHIBITION-AS-CATALOGUE

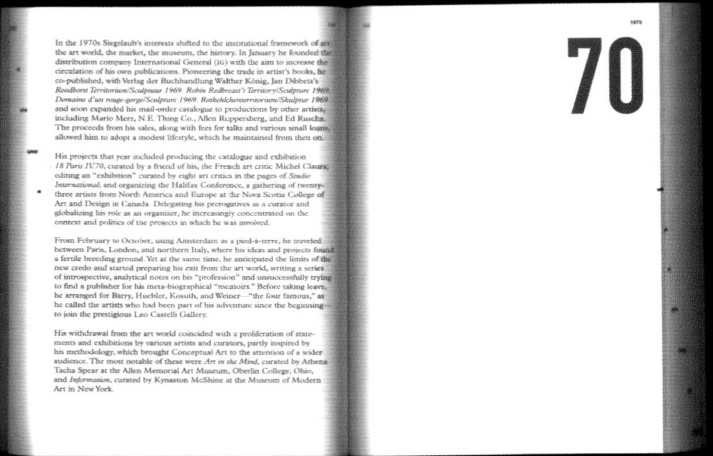

In the 1970s Siegelaub's interests shifted to the institutional framework of art: the art world, the market, the museum, the history. In January he founded the distribution company International General (IG) with the aim to increase the circulation of his own publications. Pioneering the trade in artist's books, he co-published, with Verlag der Buchhandlung Walther König, Jan Dibbets's *Roodborst Territorium/Sculptuur 1969. Robin Redbreast's Territory/Sculpture 1969. Domaine d'un rouge-gorge/Sculpture 1969. Rotkehlchenterritorium/Skulptur 1969*, and soon expanded his mail-order catalogue to productions by other artists, including Mario Merz, N.E. Thing Co., Allen Ruppersberg, and Ed Ruscha. The proceeds from his sales, along with fees for talks and various small loans, allowed him to adopt a modest lifestyle, which he maintained from then on.

His projects that year included producing the catalogue and exhibition *18 Paris IV.70*, curated by a friend of his, the French art critic Michel Claura; editing an "exhibition" curated by eight art critics in the pages of *Studio International*; and organizing the Halifax Conference, a gathering of twenty-three artists from North America and Europe at the Nova Scotia College of Art and Design in Canada. Delegating his prerogatives as a curator and globalizing his role as an organizer, he increasingly concentrated on the context and politics of the projects in which he was involved.

From February to October, using Amsterdam as a pied-à-terre, he traveled between Paris, London, and northern Italy, where his ideas and projects found a fertile breeding ground. Yet at the same time, he anticipated the limits of the new credo and started preparing his exit from the art world, writing a series of introspective, analytical notes on his "profession" and unsuccessfully trying to find a publisher for his meta-biographical "memoirs." Before taking leave, he arranged for Barry, Huebler, Kosuth, and Weiner—"the four famous," as he called the artists who had been part of his adventure since the beginning—to join the prestigious Leo Castelli Gallery.

His withdrawal from the art world coincided with a proliferation of statements and exhibitions by various artists and curators, partly inspired by his methodology, which brought Conceptual Art to the attention of a wider audience. The most notable of these were *Art in the Mind*, curated by Athena Tacha Spear at the Allen Memorial Art Museum, Oberlin College, Ohio, and *Information*, curated by Kynaston McShine at the Museum of Modern Art in New York.

1970

70

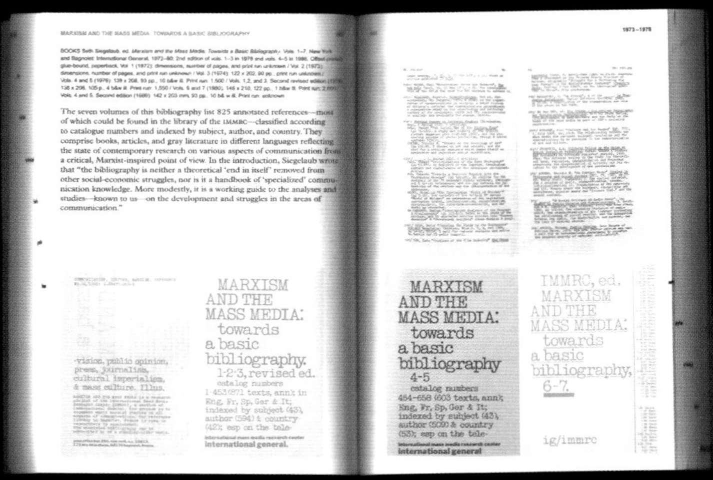

MARXISM AND THE MASS MEDIA: TOWARDS A BASIC BIBLIOGRAPHY

BOOKS Seth Siegelaub, ed. *Marxism and the Mass Media: Towards a Basic Bibliography*. Vols. 1–7. New York and Bagnolet: International General, 1972–80; 2nd edition of vols. 1–3 in 1978 and vols. 4–5 in 1986. Offset printed, glue-bound, paperback. Vol. 1 (1972): dimensions, number of pages, and print run unknown / Vol. 2 (1973): dimensions, number of pages, and print run unknown / Vol. 3 (1974): 122 x 202, 80 pp., print run unknown / Vols. 4 and 5 (1976): 139 x 208, 93 pp., 10 b&w ill. Print run: 1,500 / Vols. 1, 2, and 3. Second revised edition (1978): 138 x 206, 105 p., 4 b&w ill. Print run: 1,550 / Vols. 6 and 7 (1980): 146 x 210, 122 pp., 1 b&w ill. Print run: 2,000 / Vols. 4 and 5. Second edition (1986): 142 x 203 mm, 93 pp., 10 b& w ill. Print run: unknown

The seven volumes of this bibliography list 825 annotated references—most of which could be found in the library of the IMMRC—classified according to catalogue numbers and indexed by subject, author, and country. They comprise books, articles, and gray literature in different languages reflecting the state of contemporary research on various aspects of communication from a critical, Marxist-inspired point of view. In the introduction, Siegelaub wrote that "the bibliography is neither a theoretical 'end in itself' removed from other social-economic struggles, nor is it a handbook of 'specialized' communication knowledge. More modestly, it is a working guide to the analyses and studies—known to us—on the development and struggles in the areas of communication."

-vision, public opinion,
press, journalism,
cultural imperialism,
& mass culture. Illus.

MARXISM
AND THE
MASS MEDIA:
towards
a basic
bibliography.
1-2-3, revised ed.
catalog numbers
1-453 (871 texts, ann); in
Eng, Fr, Sp, Ger & It;
indexed by subject (43),
author (594) & country
(42); esp on the tele-
international mass media research center
international general.

1973–1978

MARXISM
AND THE
MASS MEDIA:
towards
a basic
bibliography
4-5
catalog numbers
454-658 (603 texts, ann);
Eng, Fr, Sp, Ger & It;
indexed by subject (43),
author (509) & country
(53); esp on the tele-
international mass media research center
international general

IMMRC, ed.
MARXISM
AND THE
MASS MEDIA:
towards
a basic
bibliography,
6-7.

ig/immrc

subject key

1.00 General
- 1.01 Basic Marxist Texts on Society Relevant to Communications
- 1.02 General Theory of Culture and/or Ideology
- 1.03 General Theory of Communications
- 1.04 History of Communications
- 1.05 Communications Research and Methodology
- 1.06 Bibliographies
- 1.07 Biographies

2.00 Pre-Print Communications
- 2.01 Speech

3.00 Print
- 3.01 General
- 3.02 The Capitalist Press, Magazines, News Agencies
- 3.03 The Working Class Press, Magazines, News Agencies
- 3.04 Publishing: Books, Bookstores, Libraries
- 3.05 Photography, Design, Typography, Posters
- 3.06 Miscellaneous Print Media: Mimeograph, Photocopy, Microfilm, etc.
- 3.07 Comicbooks, and Cartoons
- 3.08 The Post Office and Telegraph

4.00 Sound
- 4.01 Radio
- 4.02 Telephone
- 4.03 Miscellaneous Sound Media: Phonograph, Tape Recorder, etc.
- 4.04 Electronic Surveillance

5.00 Audio Visual
- 5.01 Television
- 5.02 Cable TV, Videotape, Video-recorders, Cassettes
- 5.03 McLuhan

6.00 Social Consciousness (Propaganda/Public Opinion)
- 6.01 Advertising/Public Relations
- 6.02 Public Opinion Polls
- 6.03 Management

7.00 Journalism/Media and Cultural Workers
- 7.01 Copyright

8.00 International Communications/Cultural Imperialism
- 8.01 Satellites
- 8.02 Multinational Corporations
- 8.03 Tourism

9.00 Cybernetics and Information Theory
- 9.01 Computers

10.00 Language, Linguistics, and Semiology
- 10.01 Content Analysis

11.00 Related
- 11.01 Mass Culture
- 11.02 Education
- 11.03 Film
- 11.04 Free Time

MARXISM AND THE MASS MEDIA: towards a basic bibliography.

1-2-3, revised ed.

catalog numbers 1-453

international mass media research center

international general.

كيف تناور:
في شكل
النصوص
وتدابير
النشر
تحرير: كيف تـ

How to maneuver:
Shapeshifting
texts and other
publishing
tactics
edited by Kayfa ta

تشكل اختيارات عموم الناشرين مشهدنا الثقافي ولا تُمثله بشكل كامل. تظهر فقط مشاريع النشر التي تنجح في تجاوز صمامات مالية وقانونية وسياسية يتحكم بها كل من السوق والدولة. اللغات والأنماط المهمشة في صناعة النشر السائدة - الأنواع المنبوذة، الموضوعات المحظورة، الذاتيات القلقة، اللغات المفرطة أو المتقشفة، غير المربحة أو المبهمة - متخلّى عنها، مدفوعة لتعمل في الظل، أو أن تعاند في إيجاد كيفية لظهورها.

يقدم هذا الكتاب مجموعة غنية من الكتابات والمشاريع البحثية والأعمال الفنية التي تنظر في ممارسات النشر المغاير، المعاصرة والتاريخية، مع التركيز على المنطقة العربية وبعض الممارسات العالمية. بدءًا من اللافتة الدعائية المرسومة باليد لترويج نشر ذاتي، وصولًا الى دور نشر مستقلة أسست لنفسها مكانة نسبية، تُظهر ممارسات النشر البديلة اتساع رقعة الممكن والقوة الكامنة في بعض مقترحاتنا المدنية الأكثر إبداعًا وجرأة.

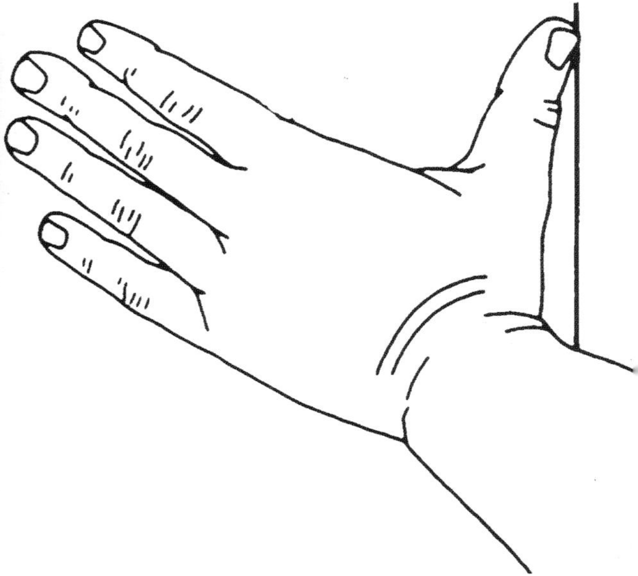

ISBN 978-9948-34-465-0

What is deemed publishable shapes our cultural landscape, but only partially reflects it. What becomes visible are publishing projects that have succeeded in passing by the multiple financial, political and legal valves governed by market and state alike. Languages and formats that are deliberately or accidentally marginalized—the snubbed genres, the outlawed subjects, the troubling subjectivities, the excessive, the minimal, the unprofitable, and the unfathomable—are aborted, pushed underground, or stubbornly persist to find a place in the sun.

This book presents a rich variety of writings, research projects and artworks that reflect on contemporary practices and histories of publishing, with a strong focus on the Arab world and resonant international practices. From the hand-drawn, self-promoting banner to the relatively established independent publishing house, alternative publishing practices show both the breadth of possibility, as well as the great strength and vulnerability, of some of our most creative and daring civic propositions.

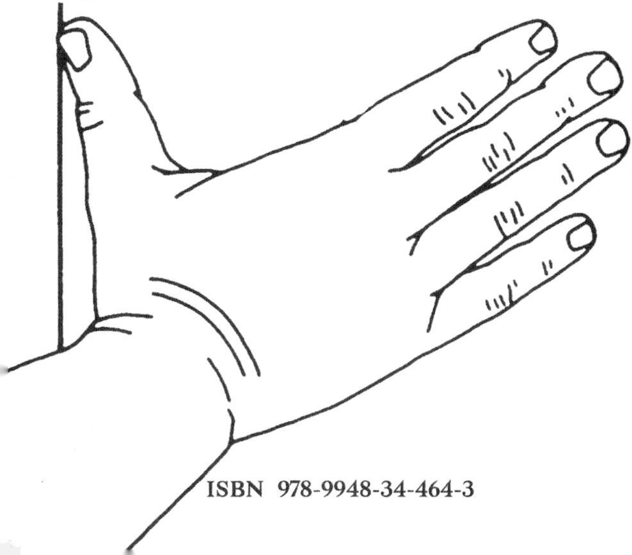

ISBN 978-9948-34-464-3

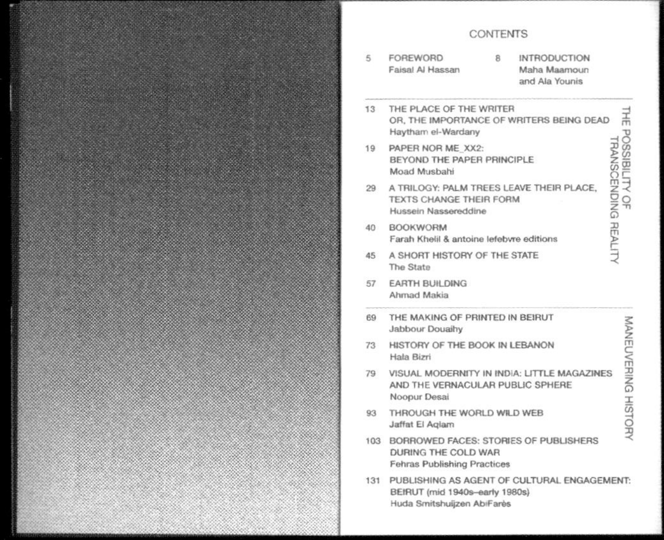

CONTENTS

المطلوبة لتحقيق حلم ساداكو وحلمه. تتداخل في صفحات الكتاب قصة ساداكو
مع تاريخ سوريا والشرق الأوسط، وطن أجداد دلول، بينما ينظر في مفاهيم
الدولة والفرد وفي مصير بلد ما، وفي الأثر المزمن لتقلبات تاريخ بلد على أبنائه.

في افتتاحية العدد الأخير في فبراير ١٩٧١، وتحت عنوان «لماذا يجب أن تستمر جاليري ٦٨؟»، دعا إدوار الخراط كُتّاب المجلة وأصدقاءها إلى أن يدعموا استمرار المجلة كصوت تجريبي وطليعي في الكتابة والترجمة والنشر، وأنه، وفقًا لرأي الكاتب جميل عطية إبراهيم، ضمن دراسة للباحثة إليزبيث كندل عن المجلة، فإن الكُتّاب الذين بدأوا في «جاليري ٦٨» انفتحت أمامهم أبواب النشر على اتساعها في المجلات الثقافية الأخرى المصرية والعربية، إلى حد أن فريق تحرير المجلة لم يجد مواد كافية صالحة للنشر لإصدار عدد بعد الثامن. كان العدد الثامن هو العدد الأخير من «جاليري ٦٨» إلى أن أتى عبد القادر حاتم وزيرًا للثقافة والإعلام أواخر عام ١٩٧١، وتوقفت عن الصدور معظم تلك المجلات الثقافية ثقيلة الظل بجرة قلم.

نحو اتحاد كُتّاب ديموقراطي مستقل

في ٤-٨ ديسمبر ١٩٦٩، عقد في الزقازيق مؤتمر أدباء الأقاليم والكُتّاب الشبان بدعوة من الاتحاد الاشتراكي لاحتواء المثقفين والكُتّاب الشبان الغاضبين بعد هزيمة ٦٧، وطلبوا من نجيب محفوظ أن يكون أمين عام المؤتمر لكنه رفض بدبلوماسية، وتولى ذلك شعراوي جمعة، وزير الداخلية وأحد قيادات الاتحاد الاشتراكي والتنظيم الطليعي الناصري. أثار هذا الأمر صدمة ودهشة الكثيرين وأشعل النقاشات الحادة في جلسات المؤتمر حيث عبّر مائة كاتب من مختلف أنحاء مصر عن رغبتهم في أن ينظموا اتحادًا للكُتّاب. لم يسمح النظام بتكوين اتحاد خارج منظومته، لكن المؤتمر أصدر مطبوعة ثقافية أدبية جديدة وهي مجلة «سنابل» التي صدرت في كفر الشيخ في ديسمبر ١٩٦٩. سعت المجلة إلى تغطية الأنشطة الثقافية من مختلف الأقاليم، وكذلك النشر لكُتّاب من مختلف القرى والمدن. وكانت تحرر بابًا بعنوان «من شرنقة النار» تنشر فيه نصوص الكتّاب المقاتلين على الجبهة في سيناء، وظلت تصدر حتى توقفت في عام ١٩٧١، ربما بسبب نشر قصيدة «الكعكة الحجرية» لأمل دنقل أو بسبب ضعف التمويل الذي حدث على إثر انتقال المحافظ المتحمس لطباعة المجلة إلى إقليم آخر.

عام ١٩٧١، وفي ظل أجواء قمعية وتطهيرية شديدة ضد اليسار والحركة الطلابية بتنويعاتها، تأسست جمعية كُتّاب الغد برئاسة إبراهيم فتحي بترخيص من وزارة الشؤون الاجتماعية ومقرها في وسط مدينة القاهرة بالقرب من ميدان التحرير تحت شعار «نحو اتحاد كُتّاب ديمقراطي مستقل». كانت الجمعية بشكل ما تعيد إنتاج طريقة العمل الشيوعي السري منذ الأربعينيات حيث كانت بمثابة منتدى نقاش عام لمنظمة ماركسية سرية هي (حزب العمال الشيوعي المصري) وكانت بالقطع علاقاتها معقدة مع الحزب، ولم يكن الهدف منها تجنيد كوادر للحزب، وكانت تضم يساريين من جماعات ماركسية أخرى، منهم الناقد عبد المنعم تليمة من التيار الثوري (المتوافق مع السادات).

صدرت عن الجمعية مطبوعات مستقلة خارج إطار الدولة، كان أولها ديوان الشاعر عزت عامر والذي سيكون من أوائل المتهمين في قضايا انتفاضة الخبز في ١٨ و١٩ يناير، عام ١٩٧٧، بعد ذلك صدر «مدخل إلى الحدائق

الطاغورية»، والذي يُعد من بواكير قصيدة النثر، كما يشمل الكتاب مانفيستو الجمعية «نحو اتحاد كُتّاب ديمقراطي مستقل»، وتذييلا نقديًا بقلم إبراهيم فتحي. ثم ديوان «وش مصر» لزين العابدين فؤاد ورواية محمد روميش «الليل.. الرحم» في ١٩٧٣. بعدها اعتقل إبراهيم فتحي، وكذلك الشاعر أحمد عبيدة، الذي تعرض لتعذيب شديد في السجن ولجلسات كهرباء في مستشفى الأمراض العقلية، واحتجز القسم الشنطة التي تحتوي على معظم أشعاره مما ترك أثرًا بالغًا عليه وأقدم، بعد الإفراج عنه، على وضع كتبه وملابسه ونفسه في حفرة بأرض بيته وأضمر النار فيها وفي نفسه فمات محترقًا. أصدرت الجمعية في أربعين وفاته كتابًا لمختارات من أشعاره مع مقدمة لصديقه إبراهيم فتحي. في نفس العام، ١٩٧٤، ظل كُتّاب وفنانون ومخرجون سينمائيون من الجمعية هدفًا للاعتقال على إثر بلاغات من يوسف السباعي الذي أصبح وزيرًا للثقافة، حتى توقف نشاط الجمعية في ١٩٧٥.

«مصرية»، العدد الأول، القاهرة، ١٩٨٠.

سيرة الماستر

ما بين عامي ١٩٧٣ و١٩٧٦، قام السباعي بتجفيف منابع اليسار المناهض لسياسات السادات من جهاز الثقافة وتطهير المؤسسات الثقافية والإعلامية، والذين كان السادات يلقب مثقفيهم وفنانيهم بـ «الأراذل». بدأ السباعي يتدخل في تحرير مجلة «الكاتب» التي كانت تصدر عن هيئة الكتاب مما دفع مجلس تحريرها من كُتّاب ومثقفين يساريين بتقديم استقالة جماعية عام ١٩٧٤. قبلت الاستقالة وأتى صلاح عبد الصبور رئيسًا للتحرير حتى توقف صدور المجلة عام ١٩٧٩. ثم بدأ يتعامل مع اليمين الثقافي عبر إعادة إحياء أو إنشاء مجلات أدبية مثل

by the editorial board of Dar al-Fata al-Arabi. After these initial contacts with the children in the camps, he set out to lay the ground for the practical design and production of the project – ultimately the only fundamental role he played in the creation of this publishing and cultural project. He wrote: "I moved on to other more practical and technical matters to lay the ground for work that would follow upon my return to Beirut. I never fathomed that this preparatory period was to be the only stretch of time I would spend on this job."[23]

During this initial period of six months in Beirut, Boullata continued his research and planning. He often met with the editorial committee, reviewing the stories that were being submitted for the potential books, and updating them on his progress. He met with local artists and writers that could become potential contributors, visited and checked on local printing facilities investigating potential paper stock and suppliers, using various sorts of paper to create mockups of books in various formats and sizes. He also made several preliminary sketches of the layouts and text compositions. He presented his work to the editorial committee "knowing that [his] suggestions were subject [to] collective approval," and he was "open to listen to any constructive input" as well as be ready to defend his decisions. He wrote: "Some of my suggestions were accepted, others were not. I had no problem with any of that."[24]

Even before Boullata had left Beirut, the stories for the books accumulated, potential writers were contacted by himself and other members of the editorial committee, and stories had amounted to approximately one hundred. Throughout his sojourn in Beirut, Boullata continued to think of practical design solutions in which "a readable text and an attractive illustration could be wedded together on facing pages to ignite the imagination of a child," to be combined "in such a way that form and content were to make up a single body."[25] For Boullata, finding writers who were interested in children's

23 Ibid. 8.
24 Ibid. 9.
25 Ibid. 11.

books was far easier than artists interested in illustrating them. In Beirut artists did not discern the difference between art direction and illustration and regarded both as commercial activities. However in Egypt, children's publishing was thriving: "[a] number of trained painters made inroads as illustrators of drawings which livened up adult weeklies" such as *Rose al-Yusuf* and *Sabah al-Khayr*, and by the 1950s, Arab children "were availed of the pioneering children's periodical *Sindibad*" and later the colored children's magazine *Samir*."[26]

Boullata believed that by the 1970s it was high time for "Arab culture to produce authors specialized in children's books that could dismantle the Kamel Kilani model"[27] of moralized and didactic 1950s classical Arabic stories. He looked for a fresh voice for the stories of the younger generation of fiction writers, storytellers and poets as potential contributors. He invited a number of young people who had not been drawing since childhood to contribute with illustrations. He wanted texts, stories, and images that could ignite a child's curiosity and fantasy. He also encouraged the artists he met to write their own stories and writers to illustrate their own stories, naming Antoine de Saint-Exupéry's *The Little Prince* as an example. He took his time selecting text, and matching them with illustrators because he believed the story and the style of illustration had to be unified. In his choices he tried to include artists and writers from various parts of the Arab world to best communicate the Arab solidarity with the Palestinians.[28] He wrote: "I saw that our pioneering project was an experimental venture, I thought we could afford to take some time to explore a new way of looking at children's books."[29]

In addition to his responsibilities as art director, Boullata illustrated three books during his six months in Beirut. One for each of the series he had created. He also designed the logo of the publishing house which was retraced from an original

26 Ibid. 12.
27 Ibid.
28 Ibid. 14.
29 Ibid. 13.

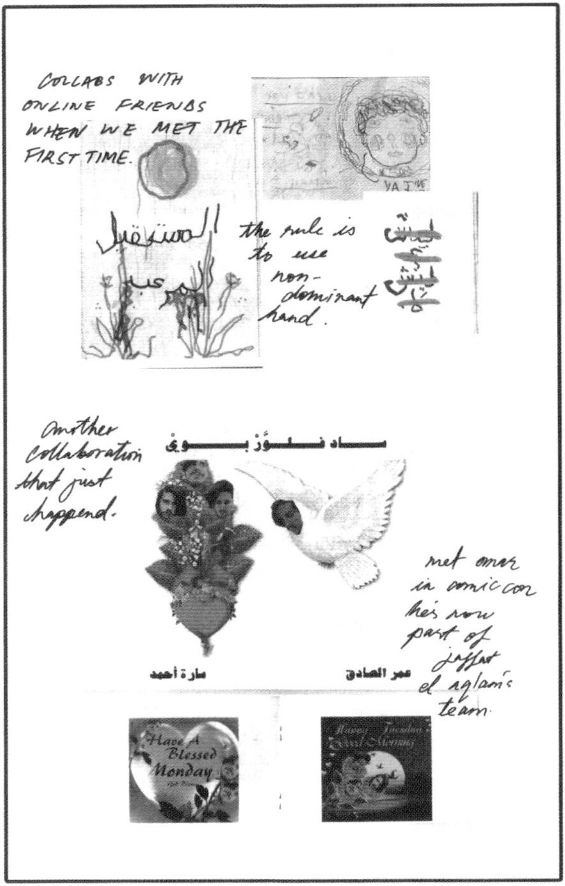
COLLABS WITH
ONLINE FRIENDS
WHEN WE MET THE
FIRST TIME.
المستقبل
المرعب
the rule is
to use
non-
dominant
hand.
another
collaboration
that just
happend.
سارة أحمد
عمر الصادق
met omar
in comic con
he's now
part of
jaffat
el aqlam's
team.
Have A
Blessed
Monday

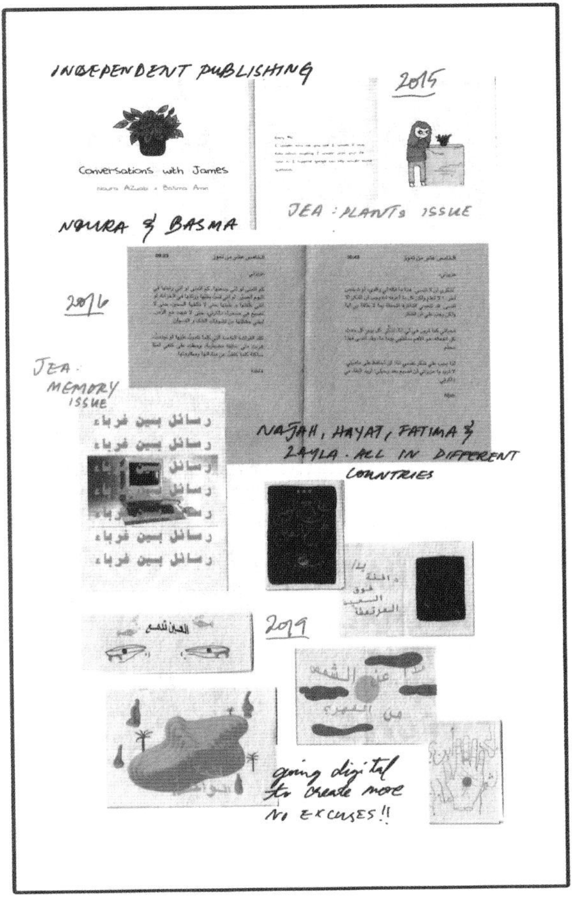
INDEPENDENT PUBLISHING
2015
Conversations with James
NOURA & BASMA
JEA : PLANTS ISSUE
2016
JEA · MEMORY ISSUE
رسائل بين غرباء
NAJAH, HAYAT, FATIMA & LAYLA · ALL IN DIFFERENT COUNTRIES
2019
going digital to create more
NO EXCUSES!!

archive books

body
luggage
steirischer herbst

Cover page
Hilde Holger, possibly photographed in the clandestine studio of artist Felix Albrecht Harta
Vienna, c. 1938–1939/Anschluss
Photo Anton Josef Trčka/ pseudonym Antios
Courtesy Hilde Holger Archive
© Primavera Boman-Behram
'...we danced and freed ourselves for some hours, from all the horror inflicted on us.' HH, memories of the hidden meetings, 90s.

1
Photo shoot, Hilde Holger at Juhu Beach, Bombay, 1944
Photo Charles Petras/Petrasch
Courtesy Hilde Holger Archive
© Primavera Boman-Behram

2
Hilde Holger, choreographer
'Apsara', Hampstead Theatre, London, 1983
Photographer unknown
Courtesy Hilde Holger Archive
© Primavera Boman-Behram

3
Hilde Holger, choreographer
'Bauhaus', Commonwealth Theatre, London, 1972
Photo Douglas Elston
Primavera Boman-Behram, costume design
Courtesy Hilde Holger Archive
© Primavera Boman-Behram

4–5
Gertrud Tenger with her husband to be, solo-dancer Werner Wachsmuth Oberhausen, late-1920s
Photographer unknown
Courtesy Gertrud Tenger Archive

6
Gertrud Tenger, 1920s/30s
Photographer unknown
Courtesy Gertrud Tenger Archive

7
Padmini Chettur
'Varnam'
Still from video-installation
3-channel video projection
16:9, 22 minutes, sound, colour, 2016

8
Padmini Chettur
'Beautiful Thing 1'
Photo Sara
Courtesy the artist

9–10
Portia Zvavahera
'Embraced and Protected in you'
Details, Oil-based printing ink and oil bar on canvas
210 x 390 cm, 2016
Courtesy of the artist and Stevenson, Cape Town and Johannesburg

11–12
Kemi Bassene
'Sedentarism in desert migratory movement'
Detail, Installation, 2016

13
Detail of court robes from late Qing dynasty (1644–1911), sent to Gertrud Tenger by her sister Edith from Shanghai, early 1930s
Photo: Arye Wachsmuth
Courtesy Gertrud Tenger Archive

14
Court robes from late Qing dynasty (1644–1911), sent to Gertrud Tenger by her sister Edith from Shanghai, early-1930s
Photo: Arye Wachsmuth
Courtesy Gertrud Tenger Archive

15
Simon Wachsmuth
'Qing'
Still from video-installation, 2-channel video projection and archival images
16:9, 24 minutes, sound, colour, 2016

16
Chaw Ei Thein
'Body to Body'
Stills from video-installation
16:9, 8 minutes, sound, colour, 2016

17–18
Jimmy Chishi
Details from the series 'Migrating Biographies',
Shadow puppets, 2016

19
Hilde Holger, choreographer, dancer
'Golem'
Vienna, 1937
Photographer unknown
Kate Berl, costume design
Friedrich Wilckens, music
Courtesy Hilde Holger Archive
© Primavera Boman-Behram

20–21
Htein Lin
'The Fly'
Performance for Art-Evict
Hackney Squat, London, October 2010
Photographer unknown
Courtesy the artist

22–23
Sawangwongse Yawnghwe
'Spirit Vitrines (Memoirs of a Shan Exile)', clay, vitrines, wax, soap, mud, felt, rice paper, holy threads, pigment, spice, water and oil, Dimensions variable, 2016

25
Caecilia Tripp
'Untitled (Lampedusa Sorrow Song)'
Offset print on paper, 2016

26
Bessora, 'The Quiet Circus of the Museum'
Original text, 2016

Back cover
Gertrud Tenger
Photographer unknown
Courtesy Gertrud Tenger Archive

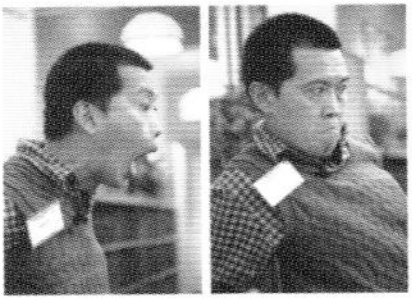

Htein Lin
'The Fly'
Performance for Britain-Burma Society meeting Medical Society, London, December 2006
Photo Martin Le Santo-Smith
Courtesy the artist

Htein Lin
'The Fly'
Performance for Art-Evict Hackney Squat, London, October 2010
Photographer unknown
Courtesy the artist

The coming to new vocabulary out of an older dance-form, and the pioneering of performance art in Burma, is similarly a missing art history of the 1990s. Two Burmese artists re-invented the comic traditional anyient dance, as a sarcastic form of 'performance art'.

In Myaungmya prison Htein Lin invented a performance called, 'The Fly'', and he first performed it there in 2001 – just once – for about 30 political prisoners. Among those watching was U Phyo Min Thein, today Yangon's chief-minister. In what Htein Lin calls the golden age in Myaung-Mya Prison he and other political prisoners – after refusing food and arguing against ill-treatment – could persuade the prison authorities to allow them to circulate freely within the prison, and they were able to carry out political commemorations, and discuss their future political strategies. 'The Fly' was based on a punishment devised by the prison guards, who asked the prisoners to catch up to 200 flies and mosquitoes with their hands each day. Among other punishments, such as the 'motorcycle', torture, confinement and beatings, described as 'a living hell' by Burmese political prisoners, the extent of absurdity of this punishment, is met with the extent of black comedy Htein Lin brings to his facial expressions, as he appears tied to a chair – perhaps in confinement – faced with a battle of driving away unrelenting. His first performance of 'The Fly' outside prison, was at Gangaw Group Show in Yangon in early 2005, and then at the Institut Français in August 2005. The images and films collected, focus on various performances of the same work.

Htein Lin held two solo shows in 1996 and 1997. He supported himself with work as a comedian, dancer and actor, and joined an 'anyeint troupe', of his friend Zarganar, of stage actors working with contemporising an ancient form of dance meant for the courts, among whose staple characters are a beautiful princess, and a buffoon. Dances are interrupted by a league of comics, who discuss between them everyday politics, in what used to be one of the only channels by which the population could critique the kings, without fear of censure. It was at this time that he made among the first works of self-conscious performance art in Burma. He combined the traditional ancient comic routines with his search for a new art language, making them pioneering experiments in performance art in Yangon. In 1996, he made two street performances, 'Plastic Age' and 'Guitarist' in the centre of Yangon.

2

3

4

5

6

body luggage
migration of
choreographic signs

Zasha Colah

'body luggage' imagines the migration of choreographic signs across borders, of body language as the signs carried on our backs, even if they are the only luggage we are able to carry. What people bring with them in situations of exigency become the basis of archives of memory—from a previously uninhabited island's search for 'oral objects' carried by slaves and indentured workers for the proposed museum 'Maison des civilisations et de l'unité Réunionnaise', to the recent 'Archivio Memorie Migranti' in Lampedusa. When on one side of the sea bodies are returned to slavery, translatable as currency, and on the other, there is time enough to frame Danish 'jewellery laws' to confiscate everything of value from those seeking refuge—then among the inalienable things carried, is body language, carried like frozen shapes within the body's own memory.

By placing history alongside artistic mutations the exhibition asks questions of how avant-garde forms transmit, or are provoked. Why does a choreographer at the centre of the Viennese dance world—forced to flee the Nazi regime within a day to Bombay carrying nothing—exchange the word 'dance' for only 'movement art'? Why does an Indian dancer re-invent classical forms in the '80s, immediately following her trial of sedition against the state? What induces an artist, after torture and years in exile, to engage in an ancient form of comic dance as a basis for pioneering performance art in Burma/Myanmar under the dictatorship of the '90s? Why does an artist consider the body parts from mass graves in Bosnia suitable for a novel non-identitarian politics of memory?

The mutation of forms, as put forward by Alois Riegl with the acanthus leaf and Aby Warburg with hand-gestures in his 'Mnemosyne' were attempts to connect the world's art histories to each other, through the lens of a detail. The works of 'body luggage' open the idea of cultural continuance amidst traumatic displacement of bodies, objects and histories, through what is carried, transmitted and recast in cultural and body memory. Paintings, sculptural and moving image works, textiles, archives of photographs and drawings, an artistic lab in continuance through the duration of the exhibition, and texts, challenge art history, seeking how its methods may be expanded to wider avant-garde use. It may be contended that turns in art historical theory have often been a forerunner to several political upheavals and post-colonial political movements.

We carry luggage when we travel, and embedded in the idea of luggage, is an idea of movement. Not of progress of a linear narrative, but of all kinds of movement, circlings, returnings, migrations, displacements, uprootings, and exile. The phrase 'body luggage' is instantaneously all that constitutes missing art history; because it imagines all the forms that are carried ephemerally, a gestalt within taut muscle, a fugitive insignia, memorised by an individual body, and difficult to mime without some migration, or transformation of the sign (in-sign-ia) itself.

2–4
Gertrud Tenger in unknown scenes 1920s–1930s
Courtesy Gertrud Tenger Archive

5–6
Gertrud Tenger with an unidentified colleague, 1920s
Courtesy Gertrud Tenger Archive

Der Stille Zirkus
Des Museums

Bessora

Tausende von ausgestopften Vögeln hockten auf stabilen Sitzstangen. Mit Genauigkeit ahmten sie eine eingefrorene Natur nach—eingefrorenes Leben, jenseits der Zeit.
Es war das Jahr 1844.
Dein Blick verweilte auf dem irisierenden Gefieder eines frei hängenden Fasans. Mit weit aufgerissenen Augen trank das einbalsamierte Tier aus einem künstlichen Teich. Stehende Wellen, eingefrorene Zeit. Wie konnten die Farben des Vogels wohl so wunderbar erhalten geblieben sein, fragtest du dich.
Dieser Vogel, weder tot noch lebendig, träumt von Zeit. Gelangweilt vom Anblick der Museumsbesucher, die gekommen waren, um ihn anzustarren, schaut er in Richtung der Verfinsterungen, verzieht sich gen Finsternis, zu Zeiten hin, in denen ihm andere Schicksale erlaubt sind.
Arm in Arm mit Juliette schlendertest du durch die üppigen Galerien Perrin. Regungslose Giraffen standen neben starren Elefanten, unterbrochene Makaken unterhielten sich mit angehaltenen Nashörnern, und überall waren Vögel. Sie sangen nicht mehr. Ein Wiedehopf tat, als würde er sich die Federhaube putzen, neben einem Baumhopf, der allem Anschein nach im Boden scharrte, in den sich fossile Käfer gruben.
Diese Überreste des Lebendigen fühlen sich ein wenig einsam. In einigen von ihnen haust die Erinnerung an ein vergangenes Leben, während andere zu einem nächsten Leben fliegen.
Juliette erzitterte vor dem ausgestopften Federvieh: Dieses wohlgeordnete Arrangement löste ein Gefühl des Friedens und der Ewigkeit in ihr aus. Hier hatte alles seinen Platz, entsprechend seines Ranges und der Position der anderen. Die seltensten unter ihnen waren von durchsichtigen Glasglocken bedeckt, als könnten sie entkommen, oder als hätte man sie vor den Gefahren der Außenwelt schützen wollen. Die Aufmerksamkeit der jungen Frau galt der ewigen Erstarrung des Wiedehopfes.

Einige Naturforscher, seufzte sie genervt, halten aufgrund der ähnlichen Federhauben den Wiedehopf für eine Lerche. Die engsten Verwandten des Wiedehopfes haben jedoch einen sichelförmigen Schnabel und bauen ihre Nester in Baumstämmen.

Die Lerche andererseits hockt nicht auf Ästen.
Ein verstorbener Mauersegler, der sich an einem Zedratzitronenzweig festhielt, schien einverstanden zu sein. Aber besonders zu freuen schien er sich nicht. Traurig bemerktest du: Diesem Vogel ist alles egal …
Ein Mauersegler, erklärte Juliette. Es ist ein Mauersegler. Was sollte ihm denn nicht egal sein?
Hier, sagte sie, befinden sich Lebewesen jenseits von Gleichgültigkeit, sie leiden nicht mehr, kein Unglück kann ihnen jemals wieder widerfahren.
Ein Schatten trübte ihren Blick. Sie hätte sich auch gewünscht, nichts mehr zu spüren. Aber sie war nicht bereit, ausgestopft zu werden. Mit einem lauten Lachen trieb sie ihre Melancholie fort und packte dich fast kühn an der die Taille.
Sie fühlte sich sehr lebendig inmitten der einbalsamierten Tiere, und du warst ein winziges Insekt im Herzen ihres Spinnennetzes. Du schämtest dich, du arme Mücke: Wie konntest du einen Wiedehopf mit einer Lerche verwechseln? Wie hattest du nur an die Gefühle eines Mauerseglers glauben können … Zukünftig würdest du, wenn du den Drang zu reden verspüren solltest, vor dem Sprechen gründlich nachdenken, um nichts Törichtes zu sagen. Du würdest nicht zeigen, wie dumm du bist.
Euer Spaziergang führte euch zu einem Schwarm Elstern. Juliette verlor sich in ihrem Geplapper: Die vier Ecken der Welt und die am wenigsten erforschten Regionen der Welt, sprudelte es aus ihr heraus, fanden sich hier durch ihre schönsten Botschafter vertreten.
Waren diese Auserlesenen nicht wunderschön? Du nahmst dieses diplomatische Ballett mit Freude und einer Beimischung von Angst wahr.
Arm in Arm glittet ihr durch die Alleen voller Menschen in eine elegante Welt: Handschuhe, Hüte, Stöcke und schwarze Kleidung; entzückt staunten sie über die Triumphe der Wissenschaft, sie bildeten sich und ließen sich unterhalten. Es ist ein Jahrmarkt der Klugheit, eine Schau der Illusionen. Mit ihrer Begeisterung stieg auch Juliettes Stimmlage, dennoch behielt sie einen belehrenden Ton, um das Inventar der nach ausstehenden Eroberungen vorzutragen: viele wilde Vögel, deren

exzentrische Gestalt die Taxonomen zur Verzweiflung trieb, da sie sich nicht einordnen ließen. Ihre Heimat war größtenteils Afrika oder Madagaskar oder Réunion. Hin und wieder schickte ihr Mann den Gelehrten einige Exemplare aus Gabun. Übrigens war es Jean-Marie gewesen, dem sie ihre Vorliebe für Vögel zu verdanken hatte, bemerkte sie mit monotoner Stimme. Sie erinnerte sich bitter daran, dass Jean-Marie immer unterwegs war, über Stock und Stein. Wohingegen du hier warst, wie die Vögel des Museums, wie diese treuen Kreaturen, die nie ihre Sitzstangen verließen.

Sie plapperte weiter über Vögel, über die wilden, deren Flügel noch nicht gestutzt worden waren: Charles Bonaparte, erklärte sie dir, Geoffroy Saint Hilaire und viele mehr, deren Namen dir nicht bekannt waren, hatten sich nicht auf den Rang der Serie, Gruppe und sogar Ordnung dieser Spezies einigen können. War der sichelförmige Schnabel, den einige hatten, dennoch nicht Grund genug, ihnen den Namen *Falculidae* zu geben? Du hörtest ihr zu. Was die Galerien anbelangte, trat allmählich eine Art Faszination anstelle deines anfänglichen Schreckens. Plötzlich erschien es dir grandios, dass Vögel unter lateinischen Beschriftungen steif und erstarrt sein könnten. Jedes Stückchen Erde hatte also seinen Platz in diesen naturalistischen Choreographien. Langsam begannst du, es zu verstehen: auch das war Teil der Erforschung: selbstverständlich Abenteuer, aber auch Inventar der Erkennung, Klassifizierung und Erhaltung. Und da irgendwo geschrieben stand, dass du einmal ein großer Entdecker sein würdest, würdest du auch diese Aufgaben erfüllen. In diesem Moment offenbarte sich dir eine andere Szene: Du entdecktest einen Mann, einen ausgestopften Mann.

Diese Kreatur war nachweislich tot (zumindest zu dieser Zeit an diesem Ort) und stand in einem durchsichtigen Käfig inmitten einer kleinen Menagerie, zwischen einer Giraffe und einem Warzenschwein.
Er war etwa zwanzig Jahre alt, hatte gesunde Zähne und definierte Muskeln, die von einer ausgezeichneten körperlichen Verfassung zeugten.

Juliette erfreute sich an der hervorragenden Arbeit, die an seiner Haut geleistet worden war. Wieder erschrakst du: dieser Mann—du könntest an seiner Stelle sein. Angstschauer liefen dir über den Rücken; du warst kurz davor, in Ohnmacht zu fallen. Juliette hingegen war begeistert: Durch die chemische Behandlung war die Haut dieses Exemplars so glatt wie die eines Babys geworden. Dieses in seinen Kasten eingesperrte Menschenmodell hielt einen Speer und ein Schutzschild in der Hand, auf einem Schild standen seine Referenzen. In den Worten einer toten Sprache wurde die Spezies benannt, zu der dieser Körper mit dem Speer gehörte: er war ein Hottentotte. Am wichtigsten ist es, keines davon zu sein, dachtest du, als du die Angst wieder in dir aufsteigen spürtest. Weder Wiedehopf noch Warzenschwein noch Hottentotte. Ob natürlich, indigen, Pistazie oder Erdnuss, du warst keines davon, du würdest nicht geschält, nicht eingesperrt werden. Deine Mutter war schwarz, zur Hälfte, aber du warst der Sohn eines Bretonen, der zu einem Viertel Amerikaner war.
Ein Schweißtropfen bildete sich an deiner Schläfe; du befürchtetest, erkannt zu werden, zum Beispiel an deinem Geruch, weil du, so dachtest du, riechen würdest wie sie, deren Geruch so stark war.
Diese Handschuhe, Stöcke, Hüte und schwarzen Anzüge: Hatten sie erraten, wer du wirklich warst?
Juliette hatte nichts von deinem inneren Aufruhr wahrgenommen und war weiterhin entzückt: ihre Freude vertrieb all deine Ängste. Durch Juliette gehörtest du bereits zu ihnen, zu den Voyeuren. Hottentotten, murmeltest du.
In deinem Mund klang dieses Wort plötzlich poetisch. Es hatte diesen bestimmten Geschmack von Abenteuer. Der Besuch ging weiter, begleitet von erfreutem Pfeifen und lobendem Gezwitscher. Ihr gingt rechts um eine Ecke, wo sich in einem peripheren Bereich ein Sortiment an Kolibris befand. Adulte Männchen dominierten in majestätischer Manier junge Weibchen; diese waren die Mütter junger Vögel, deren Zwitschern verstummt war und noch in den trockenen Ästen mumifizierter Pflanzen hing.

Eine Stimme hinter dir ließ dich jäh zusammenzucken:
Wir haben dreißig Jahre lang an diesen Szenen gearbeitet.
Aber es war nur Perrin, einer der Besitzer der Galerie.
Er war um die vierzig, doch im spielerischen Ton seiner Stimme lag eine unerwartete Naivität. Sein Dreitagebart verlieh ihm einen abenteuerlichen Charakter. Er roch nach teurem Parfüm, doch die Blütenessenzen konnten den Geruch nach Arsen und anderen Einbalsamierungsflüssigkeiten nicht übertünchen. Er war aus Galanterie gekommen, um Juliette zu begrüßen, und verbarg die Überraschung darüber, sie Arm in Arm mit einem sehr jungen Mann anzutreffen: Sie war verheiratet, er kannte ihren Ehemann, einen tüchtigen Forscher und zugleich einer von Perrins Lieferanten toten Fleisches. Jean-Marie schickte ihm häufig unidentifizierbare Vogelarten. Eine Herausforderung für Edouard Perrin, der schon seit seiner Kindheit alle Ecken der Welt bereiste—auch Neuseeland und Tasmanien. Er hatte sogar bei der Gründung eines Museums in Kapstadt mitgewirkt. Er engagierte sich unaufhörlich dafür, die dunkle Welt mit dem Licht der Wissenschaft zu erhellen und hatte auch eine Sammlung übernatürlicher Anatomien von dreizehntausend Insekten zusammengestellt. Und Edouard Perrin war auch derjenige, der einen 27-jährigen Mann ausgestopft hatte: jenes Exemplar, das du kürzlich in seinem Käfig gesehen hast und das immer noch Speer und Schild in den Händen hielt, beide darin versagend, ihn zu verteidigen.
Juliette schätzte den Einbalsamierer sehr. Er fragte sie nach Jean-Marie. Jean-Marie hat noch immer damit zu tun, seine Fabrik in Gabun zu eröffnen, erklärte Juliette. Ein resignierter Blick legte sich über Perrins Gesicht. Er versuchte zu lächeln: Die Anfänge solcher kommerziellen Unternehmen sind oft nicht einfach. Die Engländer dominieren den Handel mit den Einheimischen. Und die Amerikaner gewinnen immer im religiösen Bereich. Damit bleibt uns nur die militärische Überlegenheit …
Solange Jean-Marie Ihnen Vögel schickt, konterte Juliette.
Perrin räusperte sich und stellte fest: Gabun hat außerordentliche Vögel.

32

34

COPYRIGHT BY
CHARLES PETRASCH

Modern Dance in India.

The Hilda Holger School in Bombay is the first school in India for Central-European Dance.
This Pioneer School is mostly frequented by Europeans, Anglo-Indians and Parsees.
The latter show great interest in Western Art.
This photo has been taken on one of Bombay's most beautiful beaches.

33

35

'It was a very interesting experiment for me to work with different races, castes and nationalities, as I had Chinese, Europeans, Indians and Anglo-Indians as my pupils who were trained for the stage. I opened a studio for contemporary creative expressionist dance and advertised the school as in Europe. To my greatest surprise only men came looking around and were dissatisfied, expecting something different, as only 30 years ago dance was only performed by prostitutes.' (Hilde Holger, 'Dancing in India: struggles to found school of western art', London, written after 1948)

36

Under colonial rule, an anti-dance movement in 1892 was begun by Christian missionaries, who demanded that traditional dances be stopped, ridiculing them as prostitution. In 1910 parts of India banned Bharatanatyam dance within Hindu temples. Holger in India in the late 1930s met the main revivalists of that period, who were seeking to reinvent Bharatanatyam, after a period of forced amnesia.

32–36
Photo shoot of Holger's students at Juhu Beach Bombay, 1944
Photo Charles Petras/Petrasch
Courtesy Hilde Holger Archive
© Primavera Boman-Behram

3 €

DiE FORSCHUNGS
REiSE DES AFRiKANERS
LUKANGA
MUKARA
iNS INNERSTE DEUTSCHLANDS
GRÜNER ZWEIG Nr. 45 PACKPAPIER Nr. 7

Dem Gedächtnis Hans Paasches

und überhaupt weil uns der Lukanga Mukara antörnt, greifen wir die alte Idee der Baumpflanzung wieder auf. Das könnte eigentlich irgendwann demnächst eine ganz dolle Äkschn auf der Burg Ludwigstein geben, sozusagen eine Begegnung der heutigen Jugendbewegung mit den Wandervögeln von einst

Infolgedessen wird ein Zehntel vom Buchhändlerpreis jedes verkauften Buches für eine Baumpflanzung oder eine Steinsetzung in der Nähe der Jugendburg Ludwigstein bereitgehalten. Sind die dadurch entstehenden Unkosten gedeckt, dann wird je die Hälfte des überschießenden Zehntels der Hans Paasche-Spende und der Jugendburg Ludwigstein zugeführt werden

Der Verlag.

EIN VERSCHOLLENES BUCH!

VORBEMERKUNG:

In Hans Paasches psychiatrischer Beurteilung steht "manisch depressives Irresein". Das bewahrte ihn im 1. Weltkrieg vor der Hinrichtung wegen Landesverrats. Nie in seinem Leben hatte er ein Blatt vor den Mund genommen. Ein echter Provo, seine Happenings und Streiche würden ein Buch extra füllen. Sein Antrag als damaliges Mitglied im Berliner Vollzugsrat, die Siegesallee einzureißen, wurde leider nicht in die Praxis umgesetzt.

Zum konsequenten Pazifist entwickelte er sich in seiner Kerkerzeit, wo er in die Welt der Russen Kropotkin, Tolstoi, Gorki und auch Bakunin eindrang.

Und dann wurde er einer der ersten Märtyrer, den die Nationalsozialisten auf dem Gewissen haben. Der Alte vom Weißen Berg sagte über ihn: "Hans Paasche ist um dieses Buches Willen ermordet worden, denn Deutschland hat er damit dermaßen durcheinander gebracht, daß es entsetzlich war. 1922 haben sie ihn gekillt."

Der Lukanga Mukara ist eine einmalige Kulturkritik. Einige Jahre später erschien noch ein ähnliches Buch, der "Papalagi" von Erich Scheuermann, eine lange nicht so deutlich engagierte Schrift, jedoch von erfahrener Hand, Scheuermann lebte einige Zeit auf Samoa.
Dazu der Alte vom Weißen Berg: "Ich kenne den Verfasser des Papalagi persönlich und weiß wie das Buch entstanden ist. Das ist kopiert, das ist regelrecht, ja man könnte sagen abgeschrieben." Wollen wir hoffen, daß dies lange verschollene Buch uns helfen kann, eine neue menschliche Kultur zu entwickeln, während wir auf die inkonsequente Seichtheit eines Scheuermann gut verzichten können.

diese „Menschen" (so nennen sie sich in vollem Ernst!) haben, nicht gefällt, so antworte ich jedesmal, Du ließest „bestens danken". Das ist nämlich der Ausdruck, den sie anwenden, wenn sie sagen wollen, was in unserer Sprache heißt: „nein, ich will nicht!"

Herr der Berge, Du zürnst mir vielleicht, weil ich die hundert schnellfüßigen Boten und ihre hundert Briefbegleiter im Walde von Bukome, an der Grenze Deines Reiches zurückließ. Das mußte ich tun, wenn ich überhaupt weite Länder und Meere durcheilen und in dies Land kommen wollte. Ich mußte von dem Plan abstehen, für jeden Brief, den ich Dir schreibe, einen Boten und einen Briefbegleiter mitzunehmen. Denn man hält es hier ganz anders mit Briefen als in Deinem Lande. Bei Dir gilt es als Gesetz, daß jeder kennt: es darf nur ein Brief an einem Tage in Deiner Stadt eintreffen. Diesen bringt ein Bote, und ein anderer begleitet ihn, denn einer alleine kann nicht Briefbote sein. Wenn die beiden den Ruhiga überschritten haben, dann eilt ihnen die Kunde des Kommens voraus, und man weiß es bald darauf in Deiner Residenz. Und wenn sie endlich, nach Tagen, über den Hochpaß von Kibata hinabkommen, dann folgt ihnen eine vielköpfige Schar hochgewachsener Jünglinge, und die Trommler und Bläser ziehen den Abhang vor Kabares Hof hinab, ihnen entgegen.

Was bedeutet dagegen in diesem Lande ein Brief! Nichts! Und das darf uns nicht Wunder nehmen; denn in Deutschland gibt es Briefe, soviele wie Gras auf den Viehweiden von Mpororo. Ein einziger Bote trägt hundert Briefe auf einmal, ja jeder einzelne Mann darf Briefe bekommen, und mancher bekommt viele auf einmal. Ich sehe selten, daß jemand durch das Lesen all der Briefe zufriedener werde oder schlechter gestimmt. Und wenn er über den einen Brief traurig wird, so greift er schnell zum nächsten, über den er froh wird, und wenn er alle Briefe fertig gelesen hat, dann weiß er nicht, ob er froh oder traurig sein soll. Nur müder ist er geworden. Und unlustiger, den Acker zu hacken, das Vieh zu hüten. Wenn er überhaupt Acker und Vieh zu verwalten hat.

Du siehst schon, es ist unglücklich, dieses Volk, doch laß mich heute nicht nach den Ursachen fragen. Ich will Dir auch in den nächsten Briefen nur schildern, was ich sehe, und will erst viel später meine Schlüsse ziehen. Noch vieles habe ich Dir zu schreiben.

Riangombe, der über dem Feuerberge wohnt und mit Schnee seine Füße kühlt, schütze Dich und mich,

Deinen Diener

Lukanga Mukara.

ZWEITER BRIEF

Birkhain, den 20. Mai 1912.

Leuchtender Kigeri!

Ich bin an einem Platze, der einsam ist. Hügel mit Büschen umgeben mich. Ein See liegt zwischen hohen Bäumen, im Schilf seiner Ufer schwimmen Enten. Im flachen Wasser stehen Kraniche, und hoch in der Luft fliegen zwei Störche, die jetzt gerade aus Kitara herübergekommen sind, wo sie die Zeit zubrachten, in der es hier bitter kalt ist und Schnee und Eis mannshoch

MODES OF uses a range of research to facilitate new perspectives on a chosen subject matter.

Providing a meeting point for multidisciplinary content to be collated and published.

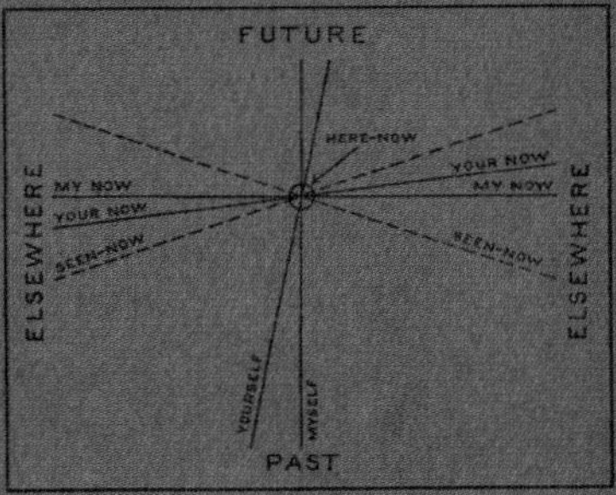

[FRONT] Theodor Holm Nelson: *Literary Machines*, 1980

[BACK] Robert Barry, Unknown

MODES OF:

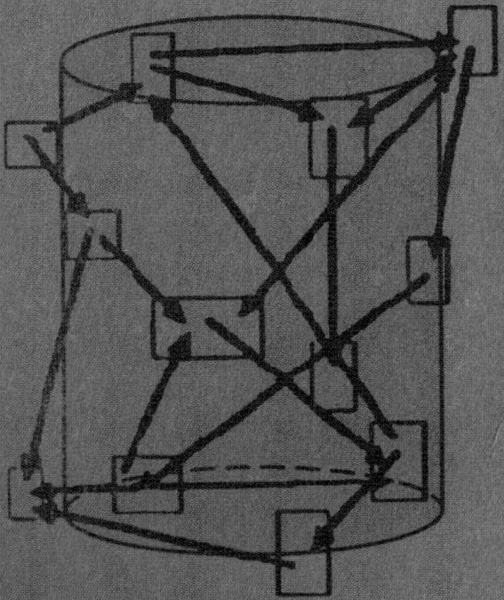

a Tin Can

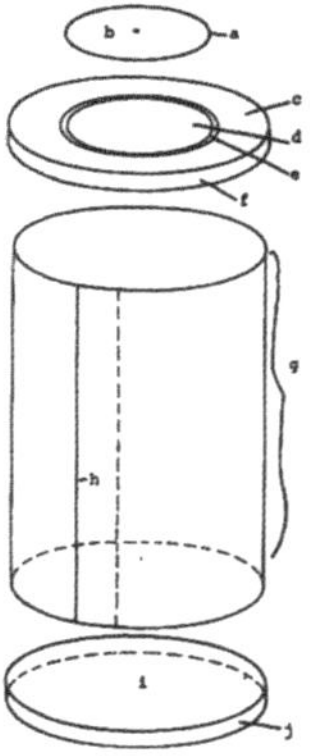

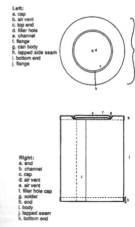

Left:
a. cap
b. air vent
c. top end
d. filler hole
e. channel
f. flange
g. can body
h. lapped side seam
i. bottom end
j. flange

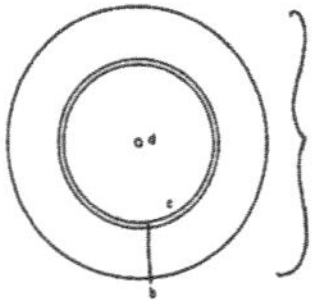

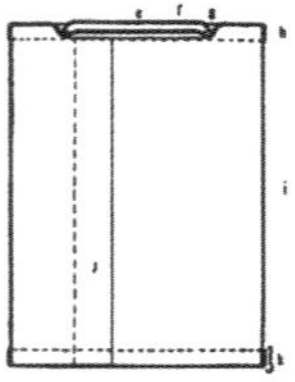

Right:
a. end
b. channel
c. cap
d. air vent
e. air vent
f. filler hole cap
g. solder
h. end
i. body
j. lapped seam
k. bottom end

1

2

THE CANNED MIRACLES OF COMMUNISM
Anna Kharzeeva / 27 November, 2015

Canned food was supposed to let women spend less time in the kitchen, and in that respect it was successful. But that's not to say it was tasty.

Nothing says communism like a bunch of colleagues with a ruler gathered over a package of canned ham from *Yugoslavia*. As Granny tells it, they're not measuring ham for entertainment - they're aiming to get equal parts of it for each member of the group. They bought the canned ham all together, as it's only sold in 3 kilo cans, which are way too big for just one person.

Ham won't be the only canned product they'll have at home. They will also have canned tomatoes and cucumbers - measured out by weight with the scales they have at the office instead of the ruler. There will also be canned tushenka - stewed meat, sprats, other types of fish, and some fruit and vegetables.

"Why did you love canned food so much?" I asked, to which Granny reasoned: "I wouldn't describe that as love. It was just available."

Even in my childhood konservy - or canned foods - had a heavy presence in our diet. One of my favorite parts of a New Year celebration was the obligatory sprats sandwich - salty and oily, with the head and tail still on, it was one of my

favorite things to eat. When I was older and went camping, there would always be tushenka and canned condensed milk - again, to me, both tasted pretty amazing.

For the Soviet dinner this week I chose to make a fish dish with potatoes and mushrooms and sour cream sauce. It's pretty easy, as all you have to do to the fish is get it out of the can and add some fried potatoes and mushrooms, sauce and cheese. We followed the recipe to the letter except for adding fish sauce into the sour cream, and the potatoes and mushrooms turned out delicious. The fish still tasted like canned fish... If I was camping, or if that was all there was, I'd eat it without hesitation, but as it wasn't, I left it mostly untouched.

Valentina Mikhaylovna, a friend of Granny's for 77 years, who was one of those people dividing Yugoslavian ham, graduated from the food university (her "third choice university") and was sent to work at a food warehouse that supplied a few local shops with goods. Each shop was only allowed a limited amount of fish (fresh or canned). Valentina saw that there were mountains left over of canned crab and cod - shops didn't want it, she was told, as they weren't real fish, nor were they cheap like some other canned fish.

A few years later, food supplies were even thinner on the ground and she regretted not

AIR BERLIN ALEXANDER-PLATZ

A like A
A like Air
A like Artists
A like Article
A like Archive
A like Altruism
A like Assem[illegible]
A like Audience
A like Argument
A like Alternative
A like Association
A like Abacadabra
A like Alexanderplatz

B like B
B like Bees
B like Book
B like Block
B like Berlin
B like Bottle-rack
B like Breakfast
B like Broadcast
B like Bent your back
like this
B like Blades to [illegible]
B like Because of [illegible]
B like there is no planet B

A like All the things I know
but of which I am not
at the moment thinking
A like A commons way
of sharing knowledge
A like An appearance
of thoughts
A like A different kind
of method
A like Another kind
of materiality
A like A day out in the
streets
A like Always on my mind
A like Anticipation
A like Anniversary
A like [illegible]iving
A like [illegible]

Spector Books
ISBN 978-3-95905-547-5
9 783959 055475

FUNKEN ZU FLAM-MEN

ARTISTS RESEARCH

ABA

10 + 1 YEARS

View from Park Inn to Alexanderstraße and Karl-Marx-Allee

TEMPO
HUT

ALTNEUBAU

ABACADABRA
INTERHOTEL
HATA
AIR BERLIN
SALON
PLATTAIR
AERONAUT
AIR-SALON.ORG

Thank you for being part of 10 + 1 years of ABA.

Adam Kleinman
Agnieszka Kubicka-Dzieduszycka
Ana Nikitovic
Andrea Hofmann
Andrea Pichl
Andrea Wiarda
Andreas Müller
Andres Villa Torres
Anna Dasovic
Anna Knoeller
Anna Schäffler
Albert Weiss
Alena Alexandrova
Aleksander Komarov
Aleksander Nowacki
Alex Reynolds
Alex Turgeon
Alexei Kuzmich
Alexander Adamov
Alexandra Leykauf
Alexandra Navratil
Alice Creischer
Alice De Mont
Alina Schmuch
Alfredo Camerotti
Althea Thaubebrger
Amanda Elena Conrad
Amelia Prazak
Ana Nikitovic
Ana Teixeira Pinto
Anders Hofgaard
Andreas Bunte
André Barc
Andrea Wieloch
Andreas Siekmann
Andreas Mueller
Andreas Siekmann
Andrei Anro
Andrew Bender
Anke Bangma
Ann Cesteleyn
Anna Chistoserdova
Anna Haase
Anna-Sophie Springer
Anna [illegible]
Anna [illegible]ckel
Anna[illegible] von Girsewald
Annika Erikkson
Annika Hauke
Annika Larsson
Antje Weitzel
Antonia Hirsch
Antonio de Luca
Anu Pennanen
April Gertler
Ariane Beyn
Armin Linke
Arts Collaboratory
Åsa Elzen
Asako Iwama
Aude Pariset
Augustin Maurs
Axel Wieder
Barbara Visser
Barbara Wagner
Bart Hofsteede
Bastien Gachet
Beatrijs Dikker
Benjamin Colle
Benjamin Deboosere
Bert Hoppe
Bertram Weisshaar
Bettina Diel
Bettina Klein
Beto Faty
Binna Choi
Bitsy Knox
Bojan Fajfric
Boris Buden
Brian Edlefsen Lasch
Camilla Laerke Mors
Camille Kaiser
Carl Zillich
Catalina Lozano
Carsten Zorn
Cassandra Edlefsen Lasch
Catherine Biocca
Cathleen Schuster
Cécile Kobel
Céline Mathieu
Charles Stankievech
Chloé Delarue
Christa Sommerer
Christel Vesters
Christina Dimitriadis
Christian-Philipp Müller
Christina Landbrecht
Christine Nippe
Christof Mayer
Christoph Baum
Christopher Jung
Cia Rinne
Clara Conza
Clara Meister
Claudia Becker
Claudia Hummel
Claudia Kugler
Clemens v. Wedemeyer
Constanze von Marlin
Cornelia Fleck
Corinna Hopmann
Cyrian Welsh
Dan Young
Daniel Rodiger
Daniela Brugger
David Dibosa
Delphine Bedel
Delphine Courtillot
Defne Ayas
Dieter Huber
Dieter Roelstraete
Dominique Hurth
Doreen Mende
Dorien Hoeksema
Dorothee Bienert
Egemen Demirci
Ehsan Fardjandiya
Elena Francalanci
Ellen Blumenstein
Elisa Rusca
Elisabeth Mohr
Elke Marhöfer
Els Roelandt
Emma Williams
Eoghan McTigue
Esperanza Rosales
Eric Peter
Erica Overmeer
Erik Lindner
Erik Smith
Erika Hoffmann
Esme Valk
Etienne Turpin
Eva Berendes
Falke Pisano
Fanny Courtillot
Federica Bueti

Ferial Nadja Karrasch
Filipa Cesar
Filippo Trentin
Florian Göttke
Florian Wüst
Frank Wagner
Franziska Sollte
Fred Dewey
Fred von Bose
Friedericke Schäfer
Gaby Steiner
Gal Kirn
Giles Bailey
Gitte Villesen
Giogiotto di Vecchio
Goeun Bae
Guido Fassbender
Grace Schwindt
Graham Kelly
Gwenneth Boelens
Hadley Howes
Hamed Kabouk
Han Le Han
Hanna Hennenkemper
Hannah Weinberger
Hanne Lippard
Hannelore Paflik-Huber
Hans Dickel
Harry Sachs
Hella Jongerius
Helmut Voelter
Heiner Franzen
Heike Klußmann
Heike C. Mertens
Hendrik Schwantes
Henrik Mayer
Hito Steyerl
Holger Schulze
Ian White
Ilka Tödt
Igor Sevcuk
Imogen Mansfield
Ines Lechleitner
Ingrid Wagner
Iris Dankemeyer
Isabelle Busch
Izabella Dabrowska
James Richards
Jan-Peter [illegible]ner
Ja[illegible]
Jan [illegible]
Jan Wenzel
Jannetje int'Veld
Jasmijn Visser
Jasper Coppes
Jayne Wilkinson
Jeanine Hofland
Jean-Pascal Flavien
Jelena Delic
Jenna Sutela
Jennifer Allen
Jennifer Lyn Morone
Jennifer Parpararo
Jeremiah Day
Jeremy Ayer
Jeroen Jacobs
Jessica Pooch
Jim Zweerts
Joachim Schmid
Joanna Warsza
Johanna Kotlaris
Jonathan Carroll
Joris Perdieus
Jos van der Pol
Jozefina Chetko
Judy Radul
Juan Luis
Julia Herfurth
Julian Klein
Julie Magnenat
Julie Sas
Jungwoon Kim
Jürg Andreas Meister
Karen Michelsen Castañon
Karen Vermeren
Kari Leigh Rosenfeldt
Karl Lydén
Karolin Meunier
Karin Anzivino
Karolin Tampere
Karsten Födinger
Kasia Klimpel
Katarina Zdjelar
Katharina Fichtner
Katharina Zimmerhakl
Kathrin Messerschmidt
Kathleen Reinhardt
Katja Gretzinger
Kato Six
Khadija von Zinnenburg Caroll

Filmstills, Ray and Charles Eames' film Powers of Ten and the Relative Siz
Things in the Universe, 1977

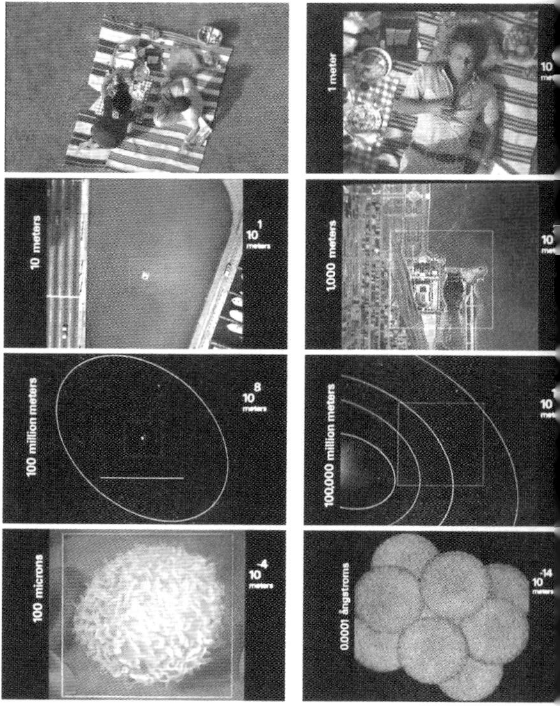

S

Salons are gatherings in the private and public sphere. ABA conceived seventy-five salons together with artists between 2009 and 2021. Each Salon was organized nomadically and highly diverse locations in Berlin were utilized as temporary platforms for discursive events.

P. 188-191	© Sorry Press
P. 192-197	© Bonnie Ginzburg Erbé, Herb Lubalin Study Center
P. 198-203	© Kunsthalle Basel
P. 204-209	© Suhrkamp Verlag Berlin
P. 210-215	© de Appel
P. 216-219	© Albatross Books
P. 220-223	© Matthes & Seitz Berlin
P. 224-225	© Himali Singh Soin (Subcontinentment Books)
P. 226-229	© Rowohlt Verlag
P. 230-233	© Grove Atlantic, Inc.
P. 234-239	© Trademark Publishing
P. 240-243	© Marek Nedelka (Letter Books)
P. 244-247	© Philipp Reclam jun. Verlag
P. 248-251	© Black Chalk & Co.
P. 252-255	© Allen Ginsberg, City Lights Books
P. 256-261	© Sternberg Press, The Showroom, If I Can't Dance, I Don't Want To Be Part Of Your Revolution, Wendelien van Oldenborgh, Julia Born
P. 262-265	© Helmut Höge
P. 266-271	© Rab-Rab Press
P. 272-279	© Stichting Egress Foundation / Estate of Seth Siegelaub, Stedelijk Museum Amsterdam, Irma Boom
P. 280-287	© Maha Maamoun, Ala Younis (Kayfa ta)
P. 288-295	© Archive Books
P. 296-301	© Packpapierverlag Osnabrück
P. 302-305	© MODES OF, Anna Kharzeeva (text)
P. 306-313	© Spector Books

Afterword

By Prem Krishnamurthy

My dear friend David Giles is an amateur author of the short form book review. Although David is definitely not a millennial, his book reviews are written in a way that younger generations might appreciate: he types them entirely on his Android phone, two thumbs tapping in alternating staccatos. This might make you think that his texts are short, something like Twitter's famed constraint of 280 characters. No, quite the opposite. They are extended, enthusiastic, even breathless investigations of a book's character, meant to express his great love of books alongside manifold philosophical musings.

Here's the review that first introduced me to his idiosyncratic form. It was sent to me as a text message—the longest and possibly best text message I've ever received. I hope you'll forgive the potentially self-aggrandizing fact that this book review was written about my first book, which no doubt endeared me even more towards David's self-assigned format:

> I finished your book this morning. I loved it. It was very readable for someone who has spent very little time thinking about On Kawara which is seriously nothing to sneeze at. You achieved something in your tone and style that I think about often or used to anyway (I haven't for a while). Is it irony? The Spanish author Enrique Vila Matas writes a lot about

this. “Irony is the highest form of sincerity,” he wrote in There is Never Any End to Paris. And “I don’t like ferocious irony but rather the kind that vacillates between disappointment and hope.” Kafka, Walzer, Vila Matas, Marias (maybe) all employ a kind of comedic irony that creates space between the subjective space of the narrator and their story or subject matter. It gives the reader space to move around in and reflect on their own experiences and their own always evolving relationship to the author, narrator, and story. I re-read the famous Paul De Mann essay on irony years ago when thinking about this and was struck again with how brilliant it was (despite the personal failings of the author of course). Is it a form of narrative self-consciousness? I wrote a bunch of stuff about this that i can no longer access mentally, at least not right now. The epistolary conceit of your essay, as a fiction in particular (since On Kawara cannot receive them much less answer them) gives you a lot of room to do this, to play around with the greetings and salutations, the indexicality of the writing, etc. It was a brilliant move. But many of your arguments and insights were brilliant as well, particularly when you zero in on the idea that his paintings were a form of lettering rather than typography, and how this assumption could go unanalyzed for so long by so many smart people, an assumption that was difficult for

people to distance themselves from in part, I imagine, because they couldn't imagine why it was important. It looks like typography, it seems to mimic typography (however imperfectly as your younger self thought) so it must be typography. And anyway even if it's not typography what difference does it make? Your essay is an extended rumination on how this seemingly subtle shift in perception creates a whole new vista of interpretative possibility, something that good philosophers do when they pick a part the arguments of their predecessors, pointing out that this seemingly insignificant logical move is not only question-begging but obscures everything interesting about the matter at hand. Wittgenstein's critique of Augustine's theory of language at the beginning of the Philosophical Investigations, for instance, and his discovery that the so-called unity of the proposition is an

enormous philosophical problem that no one has every really identified much less theorized about. How do the words in a sentence hold together as a thought when each individual word has no meaning outside the proposition/thought? I loved your playful obsessions in the book, and how you bring in analysis from self-help literature. I have heard you talking about many of the books in there for years (Perec, Foucault's Pendulum) so it was personally delightful to see how they have informed your thinking over many years. It's clear that there was much more at stake in this essay than just properly understanding On Kawara's Date Paintings, which ultimately makes it much more valuable as writing. I hope it finds a broader audience.

[original formatting retained]

David's 577 word paean does not attempt to synopsize its subject. Instead, it expresses the peculiar, personal experience of joy in reading; it follows its own preoccupations without reservation. I wonder whether the review would have received a good mark in a high school class. Many academic institutions prize so-called objectivity over excitement. Yet the fact that the writing's careening trajectory defies the calculable logic of, say, the recently released ChatGPT AI software, is what makes it valuable. This book note is willful, particular, biased, and, to my eye, beautifully bumpy. I find

David's texts brilliant encapsulations of how bibliophilic ekphrasis can, under the right circumstances, become a peculiar art form unto itself.

...

Amid the family photos, nonchalantly sexy selfies, exhibition views, dance videos, yoga ads, and artworld memes that Instagram's algorithms serve me up every day, Amanda-Li Kollberg and Siri Lee Lindskrog's "Notes on Book Design" for Berlin's Hopscotch Reading Room pop up periodically. I usually click on them to read their 2200 character captions. Although my interests run wide, I started my more mature intellectual life as a graphic designer—so things in this vein win my attention the most.

I don't think one can get away from where you come from. At least, I know that I can't. Over the past 20 years, I've called myself a curator, a writer, an exhibition maker; an artist, an organizer, a facilitator; a teacher, a learner, a performer; a tour guide, a talk show host, a karaoke MC; and more. All of these monikers might be more or less true, but recently I've come to accept that I am, at the core, a designer. It underlies how I experience and process the world.

Embracing the identity of a designer seems to come more naturally to Amanda and Siri.

They are unabashed about their love of the medium. The "Notes on Book Design" may summarize the literary aspect of the books they've chosen, but their real interest is honing in on materials, format, typography, tactility, and so on.

In this, their notes appear quite different from those of my friend David, who as a former philosopher and future novelist is obsessed with literary construction and language's nuances. Yet their project is also a kind of generative obsession, just with another focus: the syntax and structure of book design and typography. Although they may or may not type the notes on their phones (you'd have to ask them), they do go deep on the specificities of visual choices, how a certain font or particular binding or paper finish creates complex, embodied meanings. Here, these two very distinct approaches find a common ground: the quest to unravel the myriad ways in which a book means something in the world—what its printed words spark in the reader's brains and how its physical presence transmits information into the reader's hands.

Rather than trying to inhabit someone else's voice or a normative approach, Amanda and Siri burrow down deeper into their own designerly subjectivity. The serial quality of the reviews also suggests a process of learning over time. I wonder if the act of writing these book reviews one-after-another and later reviewing them as a corpus (as they have also done in order to prepare this publication) helps them to understand their own work as designers, their perspective, and their critical lens differently, sharpening the perspective that is their unique contribution.

Critics have honed their craft (and themselves) for decades by pounding the pavement, looking for shows or books to review, digesting those experiences in words, and then, thereafter, more or less consciously learning from them by writing and tweaking how they write. And then they pound the proverbial pavement again, yet with new eyes to bring to bear upon each successive exhibition or volume. It's a transformative process—a successive feedback loop that both creates observations about the world while also reflecting upon the very subjectivity that is doing the looking.

It's a little like the process of writing this text. A slightly rambling postscript for a book of book reviews that has reminded me of a simple fact: I love design, I love books, I love writing, I love the act of thinking through and with books and trying to capture their mysterious ways in a linguistic form, while also acknowledging that these beautiful books—or any given subject, to be honest—will always exceed its description by leaps and bounds. To paraphrase Kae Tempest's song "Grace", replacing only the word "love" with "books":

Make books, let me be books
Let me be booking
Let me give books, receive books, and be nothing but books
In books and for books and with books
In books and for books and with books

So thank you, Amanda and Siri, for inviting me to write this bookish, loving afterword. And I hope that you, dear reader, have lingered over these notes on book design as much as I have: finding love, of all kinds, within them. I hope they find a broader audience.

— Prem Krishnamurthy,
Berlin, 12 January 2023

Acknowledgements

Firstly, we would like to thank our publisher Onomatopee, specifically Jesse Muller and Natasha Rijkhoff. We value our collaboration, and their feedback and support have been influential on the outcome of this book.

Our friends at Hopscotch Reading Room have naturally been an essential reason that this book exists, our shared enthusiasm for the books they lovingly collect and share with the world being the kindling of this entire collaboration. We also owe thanks to Hopscotch's dedicated audience who were the initial readers of the *Notes on Book Design* series and whose occasional acknowledgement of our work was a contributing motivator for us to keep up the writing.

Prem Krishnamurthy is a spark of energy, insight, and enthusiasm—in a bar, on an archery range, on a page—and we are grateful for his thoughtful contribution to our book. We are honoured that artist John Seung-Hwan Lee—a book lover of dimensions we have yet to see matched—has captured the overflowing shelves of Hopscotch in his drawing for our back cover.

Writer and editor Bethany Rigby has proofread the manuscript and we are grateful for her time and support. We also want to thank the AGIT Cultural Centre for letting us use their scanner for hours on end.

We are grateful to all the publishers who have graciously consented to us using scans of their books. Having their trust and support means a lot. We are especially grateful to Sasha Tochilovsky of the Cooper Union/Herb Lubalin Study Center whose engagement in our project improved both the text in question and the image selection we were able to reproduce. We are also thankful that Onomatopee Projects and Etatsraad Georg Bestle & Hustrus Mindelegat have both contributed to financing the printing of this book.

And lastly—a lot of love to our partners, families and friends who have cheered us on and supported us in the process of making *Notes on Book Design* a reality.

Notes on Book Design
Onomatopee #242

Written and edited by:
Amanda-Li Kollberg
and Siri Lee Lindskrog,
Formal Settings
with written contributions by:
Hopscotch Reading Room
and Prem Krishnamurthy

Published by:
Onomatopee Projects,
Eindhoven, the Netherlands
Jesse Muller and
Natasha Rijkhoff

Graphic design:
Amanda-Li Kollberg
and Siri Lee Lindskrog,
Formal Settings
Proofreading:
Bethany Rigby
Back cover drawing:
John Seung-Hwan Lee